ALWAYS IN MY HEART

ALWAYS IN MY HEART

*The
World War II
Letters of
Ann & Coleman
Harwell*

Compiled and Edited by
Ann Harwell Wells

HILLSBORO PRESS
Franklin, Tennessee

TENNESSEE HERITAGE LIBRARY

Printed in the United States of America

04   03   02   01   00   1   2   3   4   5

Library of Congress Catalog Card Number: 00-105741

ISBN: 1-57736-187-3

Cover design by Gary Bozeman
Chapter collages by Elaine Kernea Wilson
Cover photos and letters from Ann Harwell Wells's private collection
Pastel of author by Ann Street
Line drawings in letters by Coleman A. Harwell

Published by
HILLSBORO PRESS
an imprint of
PROVIDENCE HOUSE PUBLISHERS
238 Seaboard Lane • Franklin, Tennessee 37067
800-321-5692
www.providencehouse.com

"Tonight I can see no one but you, hear no voice but yours. . . . You know that you are always in my heart and mind, but this evening you have been in this room and I have felt your hand in mine."
—Coleman A. Harwell to Ann McLemore Harwell
January 15, 1944

In memory of
Ann and Coleman Harwell

Contents

Acknowledgments

My thanks go to Andrew B. Miller, president of Providence House Publishers, and to his staff, especially Kelly Bainbridge, Mary Bray Wheeler, Elaine Wilson, and Wendy Ward, for their skill in editing, designing, and publishing this book.

I owe thanks to Gary Gore, master graphic designer, who made the initial design for the pages of this book.

Appreciation is due to friends, particularly Adelaide Davis, Kay Lazenby, Gene Allen Rose, and Ann Street, for their helpful encouragement and suggestions.

The Centennial Club asked me to read an early version of the manuscript to its members in 1995. The enthusiastic response of all who were there meant a great deal, and spurred me on to complete this book.

I am grateful to our family who have encouraged my efforts and who have supplied photographs and memories, especially Evalina Harwell Andrews, David Andrews IV, Jonathan Harwell, Robert E. Harwell Jr., Russell Harwell, William B. Harwell Jr., Morton Howell Jr., Samuel Harwell Howell, William W. Howell, and Ellen Sadler.

The late Alden Smith Sr., who, after his wife Dibbie had died, married Josephine Harwell, talked with me several times about meeting Colie overseas during the war. His sons Alden Smith Jr. and E. Dan Smith II have also been helpful.

I am grateful to my sister, Carolyn Harwell Carr, who has been enthusiastic about the publication of these letters. She and I share a cherished legacy of friendship and integrity left to us by our parents, Ann and Coleman Harwell.

My husband, Charles Wells, an accomplished writer and editor, has encouraged me every step of the way. He has been my first and most important editor.

Our children, Wyatt C. Wells II, Coleman Harwell Wells, Jenny Wells, and Ann Harwell Wells, have each read portions of these letters and have made valuable comments.

I owe a great personal debt to Ann and Coleman Harwell, whose letters form this book, and whose love for one another still permeates our memories.

I am grateful for those family members of long ago, Grandpa Harwell, Colie and Ann, Mort and Marie, Rob and Jane, Sam and Josephine and Alden. May the devotion which bound them live on in their children and in their children's children.

Prologue

"I remember as clearly as yesterday what happened," Colie Harwell wrote his wife, Ann, about her thirty-fourth birthday. "The bright Sunday morning, the excitement when I gave you the birthday 'note,' you and the girls so pleased when the final message led you to the garage and the shiny new blue car. Then the afternoon, sitting down to lunch, the phone call, 'the Japs have blasted our navy out of Pearl Harbor.'"

The day was December 7, 1941. Although this day began for the Harwells as a celebration, it ended with the United States at war.

As executive editor of Nashville's morning newspaper, the *Tennessean*, Colie Harwell rushed to the office and put out an extra at 4:30 P.M. Then came "the wire photos and more extras, more editions." "Most of all," he said to Ann, "you knew as certainly as anyone could what it meant to you and me; I would go if there was any place I could serve. You knew that before I did. You wouldn't have wanted me to do anything else."

Although he would probably have been exempted from military service by his age, job, and eyesight, Colie felt it was his duty to serve. In August 1942 he wrote his nephew Mortie Howell, then in the

Army Air Corps: "More and more local fellows are following in your footsteps. They are going in lots of three hundred almost every day." He added, with characteristic humor, "I am thinking they might even need somebody in the baldhead row before long." By February 1943 he acknowledged to a friend: "I was advised that I would be considered for the governmental officer training program, and as a result, my application for this has already gone in."

Two months later, the U.S. Army accepted Coleman Harwell into its military government program. Commissioned a captain, he left May 12 for training at the Army's School of Military Government at the University of Virginia in Charlottesville. Ann visited him twice during his three months there, first on her own, and later with their daughters, Clurie and Carolyn.

Colie left Charlottesville for overseas assignment in August, 1943, and did not return home for nearly eighteen months. Ann, Clurie, and Carolyn remained at home in Nashville, where Ann's mother, Mrs. Briggs McLemore, moved into the Harwells' guest room to assist in running the household. During this time, Colie and Ann communicated only by letter, telegram, or cablegram.

In some ways, life for the Harwell family went on as it had before. Ann continued her community activities—ranging from being chairman of the Junior League Home for Crippled Children to membership in Westminster Presbyterian Church, where the Harwell clan worshiped. She raised money for the Red Cross, and she joined the Gray Ladies, who provided volunteer services at Thayer Hospital.

The little girls, Carolyn, four, and Clurie, seven, had their own routines. In the summer, they went swimming or played with friends and visited family. When the fall of 1943 came, Carolyn entered kindergarten at Overbrook, while Clurie became a second grader at Parmer School.

With Colie away, Ann worried about the cost of living. In taking a leave of absence from the *Tennessean*, Colie traded his editor's salary for army pay. To augment this, he arranged for Ann to draw on his funds at Neely, Harwell & Co., the family wholesale dry goods business founded by his father, Sam K. Harwell Sr., and now managed by his older brothers, Sam Jr. and Rob. If she needed assistance, particularly about money, Colie suggested that Ann turn to the family. "If any considerable amounts are necessary and you are hesitant, feel free to discuss them with Father, Sam, or Rob. I know sometimes they seem rushed, but faced directly, any of them can give you the best of advice—and they are all fully aware of my finances."

Always a frugal manager, Ann planted a victory garden and preserved her own vegetables and fruits. "Grandpa brought us some apples from the farm—and Mother and I spent Saturday morning canning applesauce," she wrote Colie in August. "Our tomatoes are not so good now—so I'm going to buy a bushel and put up more. It's a slow, hot process—but how beautiful that basement cupboard is beginning to look!"

Ann could not have maintained their house and its two surrounding acres without the people who worked for her. The most dependable was Archie Buchanan—cook, houseman, occasional yardman, and babysitter. "He is like the old family retainer. Everybody else drops by the wayside and he stays on," she wrote Colie. Other household employees in 1943 included Mayola, cook and maid, and Lilybird, laundress. Part-time workers assisted in the yard. Inevitably, some of the help quit, leaving Ann in considerable "domestic upheaval," as she put it.

After Colie left Charlottesville for overseas, Ann had to make decisions about the children, the house, the servants, and the family's finances on her own, since Colie's advice was almost inaccessible. It took at least two weeks for her letters to reach him and two more for his to get back to her.

Colie's family rallied around Ann and the children. Though a plain-spoken, no-nonsense man, Sam K. Harwell Sr., seventy-nine, was sensitive to Ann's situation and respected her. He wrote to Colie in September: "This is a case like the old-fashioned War between the States when the mothers of children have big responsibilities, which they seem to handle quite well." Sam Jr., his wife, Josephine, and their children, Evalina, Leila, and Sambo, lived a few doors from

Grandpa Harwell on Harding Place, only a mile from Ann and Colie's home on Belle Meade Boulevard. They visited, took her out to dinner, and telephoned frequently. "Your family has been marvelous in making me feel they are standing behind me," she wrote Colie in October. "I don't know how I would get along without them—not that they do so much—though they do plenty—but I know they are there if the need should arise."

Rob Harwell, his wife, Jane, and their sons, Robin and Jonny, lived in Williamson County on Rolling River Farm. They too felt responsible for Ann and her girls. Soon after Colie left Nashville, Rob wrote to him, "I am still waiting to be called on for any services which I can render you or your family. I am sorry that we are so far away from Belle Meade, where we can't see them daily. However, with our situation as it is and the complications with gasoline rationing and busy days on the farm, it seems almost impossible for us to get to Belle Meade as often as we would like."

Marie and Mort Howell were living with her father on Harding Place, where their sons, Mortie and Sammy, visited when on leave from the Army Air Corps. The Howells also did their part to support Colie's family. "The girls always enjoy Mort enormously," Ann wrote Colie. "All the men in the family put themselves out more for the children now that you are away."

"You will never really know how proud I am of you," Rob wrote Colie in August 1943. "It seems to me that under the circumstances it took great courage to give up such a grand job situated as you were both in business and at home. . . . Those of us who are out often dream of the opportunities which we will miss, and which probably make us feel so very proud of those like yourself, who have had the courage to break the home ties and go into the service."

———

Colie Harwell belonged to the School of Military Government's fourth class, whose 150 members trained at Charlottesville from May 1943, until they graduated in August. Several of them, like

Colie, had come from civilian life, leaving substantial positions to enlist. Others were professional soldiers. Some had served in World War I. "An impressive number wore campaign ribbons and decorations representing prior service in this and other wars or stations,"[1] reported the *Fourth Classbook*. The class also included officers of other Allied armies.

Classes met in the university's law school building. Officers studied in the library, while a fraternity house became the officers' club. "The citizens of Charlottesville could not have been more hospitable," reported Steve Mavis in his "Reminiscences." "All officers were granted temporary memberships in the elegant and historic Farmington Country Club. However, officers were required to secure their own rental quarters in either hotels or private homes."[2]

The School trained its students to reestablish local governments overseas once the military had liberated the areas. Courses included international law, government, economics, and communications, as well as Army policy and rules, for, as a reporter for the *New York Times* noted, "These essentially civilian experts [had to be taught] to fit into the framework of Army organization and methods."[3] As did many others in his class, Colie Harwell studied German.

After leaving Charlottesville in August 1943, Colie was assigned to Fort Patrick Henry in Virginia, then transported to North Africa, where he spent approximately a month at the Military Government School there.

From October through November 1943, he was assigned to Headquarters, Allied Control Commission, in Palermo, Sicily. In December, he moved to Naples, Italy, and served until March 1944 as Public Relations Officer (PRO), Allied Military Government (AMG). From March until the end of his overseas service, he served as a spearhead Civil Affairs Officer (CAO) with AMG in the British Eighth Army, and, with his associates, moved into small Italian towns to restore order. As Rob Harwell put it to Colie, "After the battle is over, your work is just beginning."

The war for the United States began on December 7, 1941, with the bombing of Pearl Harbor, which crippled the American Pacific fleet. Immediately thereafter, the United States declared war on Japan, Germany, and Italy. By May 1943, British and American troops had defeated Axis forces in Tunisia, North Africa, where they had captured 180,000 German and Italian prisoners. Turning north to Italy, Allied forces invaded Sicily in July, clearing the land of German and Italian soldiers who retreated to the mainland. Since it was the first part of an Axis country to fall under Allied control, Sicily became the first mission for Allied Military Government.

The fall of Sicily triggered the overthrow of Mussolini. Though Marshal Pietro Badoglio, the new Italian leader, had secretly entered negotiations to join the Allies, the Germans anticipated him and quickly seized control of much of Italy. Thus, when the Allies invaded Italy in September 1943, they encountered fierce resistance from the Germans, while Italians of almost every political stripe professed eager friendship for the Allies. Colie Harwell and his AMG compatriots were to find that most citizens disavowed any connections with former Fascist or Nazi leaders.

"It is necessary sometimes to brace myself and realize that in the normal course of the day I am living things I never dreamed of," Colie wrote Ann in 1944. Ann learned most of the details of Colie's work only after the war, since censorship forbade him from revealing in his letters where he was or what he was doing. Yet he wrote fascinating letters, telling her what he could, speaking of the people he met, painting word pictures of his fellow officers, and of the Italians with whom they worked.

Colie had a knack for running into old friends—in Charlottesville, North Africa, Sicily, and Italy. Some came from his alma mater, the University of the South at Sewanee, some from family or newspaper connections, others from his years in New York or Nashville. He found Harry Cain, a Sewanee friend, in Charlottesville and again in Italy; John Whitaker, also from Sewanee and now a war correspondent, appeared from time to time; Alden Smith, a Nashville friend, turned up over and over. There were many others, all reflecting his ability to make friends at every turn.

———————

Nashville in 1943 was a prosperous southern city of about 170,000 people which had fully adapted to the war effort. Camp Campbell, near Clarksville, and Camp Forrest, in Tullahoma, had brought the military to the area, as had the Smyrna Air Field. Don H. Doyle, in *Nashville Since the 1920s*, noted that "the open, hilly land and mild climate of Middle Tennessee made it an ideal location for army maneuvers, which brought some 600,000 soldiers to the environs of Nashville in 1943–44."[4]

Thayer Military Hospital, built in 1943, provided opportunities for those like Ann Harwell, who volunteered there as a Gray Lady. The Army Classification Center on Thompson Lane "classified thousands of recruits in the flying services," reported Doyle, and "was later converted to a convalescent hospital for wounded air force soldiers and, finally, served as a demobilization center at the end of the war."[5]

In 1939, a California company, Aviation Manufacturing Corporation of California (AVCO), had announced plans to build a large airplane manufacturing plant (Vultee Aircraft), near the Nashville airport, newly named Berry Field. Fortunately, the Tennessee Valley Authority (TVA) had just come to Nashville. "Because of the availability of raw materials, of inexpensive TVA electric power and cheap labor nearby, Nashville was a promising site for the war industries boom."[6] However, military demand for industrial supplies created a scarcity for civilian use, leading to drives to collect materials like paper and scrap metal. Clurie and her classmates at Parmer school participated in many such drives. The necessity for food led the government to institute food rationing, which, in turn, pushed individuals like the Harwells into growing their own vegetables in victory gardens.

Although a center of the war effort, much of Nashville maintained its prewar lifestyle. Ladies shopped at fashionable Grace's, the expensive Weinberger's, or at Rich-Schwartz. The department stores included Cain-Sloan, Harveys, and Castner-Knott's. In 1944, Loveman's advertised a handsome woman's suit for $59.95, while Davitt's for men had a fine Knox hat for $10.00.

The Harwells usually ate at home or as guests in the homes of others. They occasionally dined out at the Belle Meade Country Club, sometimes at Sherrie's on Harding Road, downtown at Kleeman's where chicken and egg bread were specialties, or at the Hermitage Hotel. When in town for shopping or for doctors' or dentists' appointments, they might have lunch at Mitchell's, which specialized in luscious candies. They went to the movies downtown at the Fifth Avenue, Knickerbocker, Loew's, Paramount, and Princess theaters, or to neighborhood cinemas such as the Belle Meade, Belmont, and Melrose.

The *Tennessean*, which provided "Home Delivered Subscriptions" for a quarter a week, carried war and local news but also covered social happenings and had a ration coupon calendar. Among its comics, or "funnies," were "Blondie," "Smilin' Jack," and "Li'l Abner." Radio stations WSM, WSIX, and WLAC listed their daily programs in the paper, including the early morning "Breakfast Club," the popular "Superman" and "Gangbusters," and Saturday afternoon's broadcast of the Metropolitan Opera, which often drew Ann to the family radio. Want ads pleaded for female waitresses, dishwashers, cooks, and nursemaids, while also seeking male war plant construction workers, farm workers, salesmen, and railroad porters.

Nashville's Union Station, built in 1900, enjoyed its heyday during World War II. Regularly crowded with soldiers, sailors, and their families, it was often a starting point for those like the newly commissioned Captain Coleman Harwell as they set off for war. Soon after boarding the Pan-American train there for Charlottesville in May 1943, he wrote his first letter to Ann. "The trip starts well enough—good lunch without delay. Sat with a young sergeant and we chatted a good deal."

Such pleasantries filled many of the letters which he and Ann wrote in the months that followed. But their expressions of love for one another overlaid the recounting of the matters of everyday living.

"I know how much greater has been your burden," he wrote to her on her birthday in 1944, "but do as you always have done, keep your chin and back straight—wish just enough, but not too much—remember always that I love you with all my heart, that my one hope and dream is to be with you again."

Most of Colie's letters appear to have been preserved, as have Ann's, though her letters from the summer of 1943 have not been located. Included here are portions of their letters, which have been edited in the interest of space limitations. Selections from other family letters give background, as do letters to and from other individuals. Colie's private diaries and journals, kept in 1943 and 1944, have provided valuable source material.

1. *The Fourth Classbook,* 11.
2. Stephen F. O. Mavis, "Reminiscences of Allied Military Government Under Two Flags in Sicily-Italy (1943–1947)," (circa 1982), 28.
3. Harold Callender, "Trained to Govern," The *New York Times Magazine* (2 May 1943), 10–11.
4. Don H. Doyle, *Nashville Since the 1920s* (Knoxville, 1985), 113.
5. Ibid., 110.
6. Ibid., 112.

Carolyn, Coleman Harwell, Ann Harwell, Clurie, and Sam Harwell Sr. at the home of the Sam Harwells Jr.

The Harwell Family

Samuel Knox Harwell Sr. ("Grandpa"/"Father") (born 1864) founded Neely, Harwell & Company, a wholesale dry goods firm located on Nashville's public square, in 1911. He had grown up on a farm in Giles County, Tennessee, where, at 16, he had begun his career as a merchant. In 1943, he lived on Harding Place in the home which he and his wife Leila McClure Harwell built shortly before her death in 1929. Although no longer working full-time in Neely, Harwell, he continued to go to the store every day, where he sat by the front door greeting customers and employees. Two of his brothers, H. R. Harwell ("Riggs") and W. E. Harwell ("Judge"), lived in Cornersville, Tennessee. In addition to his mercantile interests, Sam Sr., and his children owned and managed several farms in middle Tennessee. Sam K. Harwell Sr.'s children were Marie Harwell Howell (b. 1893), Samuel Knox Harwell Jr. (b. 1900), Robert Ewing Harwell (b. 1903), and Coleman Alexander Harwell (b. 1905). Another son, Goodrum McClure Harwell (b. 1898), died of tuberculosis in 1916.

Marie Harwell Howell ("Marie"/"Sister") had graduated from Nashville's Ward Seminary for Young Ladies in 1911. She was married to Morton Howell in 1916. She and Mort rented out their home, "Deerwood Cottage," on Jackson Boulevard and lived with her father in his home on Harding Place after the death of Mr. Harwell's second wife, Evalina Douglass Harwell ("Miss Evie"), in 1938.

Morton Boyte Howell ("Mort") (b. 1887) was an agent for the Travelers' Insurance Company. He had received a bachelor's degree in civil engineering from Vanderbilt University in 1911.

Marie and Mort Howell's children were Morton Boyte Howell Jr. ("Mortie") (b. 1919) and Samuel Harwell Howell ("Sammy") (b. 1924).

Samuel Knox Harwell Jr. ("Sam") was a partner in Neely, Harwell, and Co., where he was responsible for the sales force and for buying fabrics and linens. Having graduated from Nashville's Duncan School in 1917, he attended Davidson College from 1917 to 1919. He received a bachelor of science degree from the University of the South at Sewanee in 1921.

Josephine Douglass Harwell ("Josephine"/"Jo") (b. 1904) was married to Sam Harwell Jr. in 1926. She spent her childhood on a farm on Cage's Bend Road near Gallatin, Tennessee, and later moved with her family to Murfreesboro. She graduated from Agnes Scott College in 1925.

Sam and Josephine Harwell's children were Evalina McClure Harwell ("Evalina") (b. 1927), Leila Harwell ("Leila") (b. 1931), and Samuel Knox Harwell III ("Sambo"/"Buddy") (b. 1935).

Robert Ewing Harwell ("Rob") was a partner in Neely, Harwell, and Co., where he was general office manager and credit manager. He received a bachelor of science degree from the University of the South at Sewanee in 1922 and attended Yale University from 1922 to 1923.

Leah Jane McKelvey Harwell ("Jane") (b. 1909), a native of Youngstown, Ohio, was married to Rob Harwell in 1933, having

Rob Harwell, Sam Harwell Jr., Sam Harwell Sr., and Coleman Harwell on the porch at Harding Place.

met him when she was a bridesmaid in the wedding of Ann and Coleman Harwell.

Rob and Jane Harwell's children were Robert Ewing Harwell Jr. ("Robin") (b. 1935) and Jonathan McKelvey Harwell ("Jonny") (b. 1940). Rob and Jane were expecting a baby to be born in the fall of 1943.

Coleman Alexander Harwell ("Colie") graduated from Peabody Demonstration School, and then from the University of the South at Sewanee in 1926. He studied writing in the graduate school of Columbia University from 1926 to 1927. He was a reporter, city editor, and managing editor for the *Nashville Tennessean* from 1927 to 1931, when he joined the staff of the *New York World-Telegram*. After marrying Ann McLemore in 1932, he and Ann lived in New York. In 1937 they returned to Nashville, where Colie became executive editor of the *Tennessean*. He remained in that position until taking a leave of absence in May 1943 to serve with Allied Military Government.

Throughout Colie's time in the service, *Tennessean* publisher Silliman Evans retained his name on the masthead as executive editor.

Ann McLemore Harwell ("Ann") (b. 1907) was born in Nashville, the daughter of John Briggs McLemore Sr. and Annie Williamson McLemore. Her family lived in Nashville until 1923, when they moved to Johnson City, Tennessee, where Mr. McLemore became president of Model Mill Company, Inc. She graduated from the Baldwin School in Bryn Mawr, Pennsylvania, studied two years at Randolph-Macon College in Lynchburg, Virginia, and graduated from Smith College in Northampton, Massachusetts in 1929. She married Colie Harwell in 1932, and in 1934 received a master of arts degree in philosophy from Columbia University.

Colie and Ann Harwell's children were Ann McClure Harwell ("Clurie"/"Lolly") (b. 1936) and Carolyn Briggs Harwell ("Carolyn") (b. 1939).

Annie Williamson McLemore ("Mrs. Mac"/"Mother Mac"/"Anne") (b. 1882), mother of Ann Harwell, had been a widow since the death of her husband, John Briggs McLemore Sr., in 1931. Mrs. McLemore grew up in Culleoka and Columbia, Tennessee, and attended Mary Baldwin Seminary in Staunton, Virginia. Her brothers George Williamson, M.D., and Robert Williamson and her sister Martha ("Mattie") Brownlow lived in Columbia, where she often visited.

John Briggs McLemore Jr. ("Briggs") (b. 1914), brother of Ann Harwell, graduated from the Asheville School for Boys in Asheville, North Carolina. He received a bachelor of arts degree from Yale University in 1937, and a bachelor of laws from the University of Virginia in 1940. In 1943, he served as administrative assistant to the Director of the U.S. Office of War Information and was based in Australia.

CHAPTER ONE

The Adventure Begins

On May 12, 1943, as a newly commissioned captain in the United States Army, Colie Harwell left Nashville by train on his way to Charlottesville, Virginia, and the School of Military Government.

Colie to Ann
Aboard the Pan-American train
Wednesday, May 12, 1943

My Dearest—

Charlottesville, the army, war, seem very unreal this bright beautiful spring day. The real things are you, the girls, home—those only are in my heart, they alone are real and will last always for me.

The trip starts well enough—good lunch without delay—imagine my ordering fish! Sat with a young sergeant and we chatted a good deal—hope that isn't upsetting to military dignity. Had a brief nap and am catching up on my reading.

You were marvelous about everything in my going away, just as you have been perfect every minute of our wonderful years together. Yours now is the bigger job—as it always has been in so many ways.

Captain Coleman Harwell.

I hope you will keep busy, not to exhaust yourself, but to keep the scenes shifting. Write me as many details as you can—I'll try to do the same. Every thought will be aimed at the time we'll be together again. I wish I could say all that's in my heart—it would be all about you. A kiss for the girls, love and appreciation to your mother, regards to Archie and Mayola.

With my heart entirely,
Colie

Colie to Ann

Charlottesville
Thursday, May 13, 1943

My dearest—

I am ensconced on the premises of Miss Mary Lewis's establishment on Madison Lane. She has two red brick buildings and houses many students and a number of officers. Miss Lewis apparently holds continuous front porch court with a Saint Bernard that never moves except to growl.

Devotedly,
Colie

Colie to Ann

Charlottesville
Friday, May 14, 1943

My dearest one—

Last night at supper I found Capt. John W. Taylor, my old friend. He is a student here too, and I am delighted, for John W. was always one of my favorite people. He mixes well, likes about everything commonplace that I do, and still is a brilliant fellow. We had lunch together today and spent the afternoon walking over the grounds and filling out questionnaires. They give you dozens of them—asking every question you've ever answered before, writing your serial number ninety-seven times, and on and on. John says they are intended for the bureau created to lose records. John is a friend of Major Washburne, whom I met yesterday, and says he is a most remarkable man, having written much on European education.

Also notice among list of "scholars" the name of Harry Cain. He went to Sewanee—is now mayor of Tacoma.

Your devoted husband,
Colie

Colie to Clurie and Carolyn

Charlottesville
Saturday, May 15, 1943

Dear girls—

I miss you both very much. I have the picture of you in your Indian suits on my dresser with a picture of Mummy. I like it here and hope to learn many things that may help me serve our country better. I know you are doing your part by helping Mummy and Grandmother every way you can. I love you very much.

Daddy

Colie to Ann

Charlottesville
Wednesday, May 19, 1943

My dearest—

I might rely on military terminology to report today's news from the School of Military Government—"The situation is fluid." That is what they say when they don't know what is going on.

I must be learning something—they are throwing a complete military and historic education at us. We have eighteen books assigned already, ranging from technical manuals to the Hunt report on occupation which I heard one rapid reader say required eighteen hours of reading. We stay at meal tables about five minutes after finishing, then everybody heads for quarters or the library. One man remarked today that this is the hardest of all army schools—even the War College.

Devotedly,
Colie

Clurie and Carolyn in their Indian suits.

Colie to Ann

Charlottesville
Saturday, May 22, 1943

My dearest—

It is Saturday night and I am thinking of you and Clurie and Carolyn—of home—how much I miss you. The inspiration of love and the beauty of home become more real, perhaps, when you are separated from them. But, deep in my heart and memory, you and all that surrounds you in our home and in our love these many brief years are so real that actually there does not seem to be a separation. Many times in these years, I have said to myself, "no man could want more, none could deserve so much." Nor were those moments

Ann Harwell.

fleeting; my constant knowledge of your love—your care and consideration, your respect and loyalty in all things—have long been alive, not any less tonight because I am miles away from you.

When I say I love you, as I do tonight and as I have said many times but never enough—I am thinking of all this. I could never put "all this" in words, so I rely on those we understand. When I hold you in my arms, or write from a thousand miles away, and say I love you, only you and I know what I mean. The days, the nights, the moments, the hours, the years, all are in those words.

I love you, my dearest, with all my heart.

Devotedly,
Colie

Colie to Ann

Charlottesville
Saturday, May 29, 1943

My dearest—

Tonight Maj. Washburne and Col. Melberg, our section chief who lives with Maj. Washburne, are asking John W., Harry Cain, and one or two others over for a bull session.

I am meeting more and more men. A few are:

Lt. Col. Junius Smith, three years in Washington war work in the office of the Under-Secretary and then the supply branch. He is brusque in his manner but with a fine sense of humor.

Maj. John Clarke from Chicago, a bond man who knows Cale Haun and all the Equitable Securities crowd.

Col. Hamilton, a regular Army Britisher, who has that English appearance of diffidence, but has a sharp mind and knows how to get things done.

Col. Donovan, short, stocky, eager, Irish, with years of Indian riots behind him.

Maj. Straus, of the Macy family, a bright and pleasant young man.

Capt. Dickson, a tremendous former University of Chicago football player, who coached at Princeton then at Michigan, and is now dean of Hamilton College, in N.Y.

The work is beginning to come out of the incubator stage and assume reality. We indulge in bull sessions about an hour long when working on a class assignment. Those are enlightening and make the work more real; also we are having splendid lectures from men who have had actual field experience.

My personal life as to details goes along all right—the negro janitor is helpful—wakes me at 7:00 each morning, sends out cleaning; the maid does my laundry well at reasonable prices. Eating at Mrs. Graves's is a big help as the food is good and sufficient. There are about twenty-five officers in the special room set aside for us, eating at two long, narrow tables. For lunch, the ladies of St. Paul's Episcopal Church serve sixty officers on a weekly ticket basis.

Your devoted,
Colie

Colie to Ann

Charlottesville
Friday, June 4, 1943

My dearest—

There is general relief that we have some slight let-up over the weekend because the class generally was beginning to droop. I noticed this especially among the older men. Tomorrow, with the exception of German, the day is given over to hearing reports from sections on their first problem. I'm glad to be on the coordinating committee of our section this time. We have to work hard on the final report and submit it before the whole class tomorrow.

Do you feel you can come up next week? I very much hope so but do not know how to advise you. When you come, I'd suggest you bring a dinner dress just in case and a swimming suit, as you might want to go out to the Club during the day.

How are the girls? Give them both my very special love. My love too to your mother for being your mainstay. And high regards to Archie.

Devotedly,
Colie

CHAPTER TWO

Life in Charlottesville

Ann Harwell arrived in Charlottesville on June 12, in time for Colie's birthday on the thirteenth, and stayed ten days.

Colie to Ann

Charlottesville
Thursday, June 24, 1943

My dearest—

Your visit was wonderful for me—It was marvelous just to know you were here and reachable.

Devotedly,
Colie

Colie to Ann

Charlottesville
Thursday, July 1, 1943

My dearest one—

Today I found a letter from Sam saying he had just talked with you, a copy of Sewanee alumni news, and the paper. For a half hour I made contact with the world again. Being reoriented, I picked up the most prosaic of chores, and balanced my bank account. I've often

11

thought how remarkable it is that auditors can take dry figures and make them come to life. Today's experience made that clear to me. Checking over my accounts I saw names and numbers that made my life real. With groceries, garden seeds, Blackout [the dog] recovered from his sickness because of Doc Bohannon, little girls' dresses—and you! So I wanted to write to say how much I love you and miss you, and how thankful I am for you. It doesn't seem entirely fair for you to have all the work on your shoulders there at home. But there it is, and although I'd give anything to put my arms about those shoulders, I am thankful they bear so sturdily the burdens forced on them now.

My heart has been full in recent days with missing you and the girls. I wonder if we shouldn't plan to take a place here for the last month. Perhaps it is not fair to close this reality to the girls—would it make this chapter in life more real for them, if there were a memory of Charlottesville and us here? You could close the house and perhaps even bring Mayola—would it be too much for you?

Your devoted husband,
Colie

Colie to Ann

Charlottesville
Sunday, July 11, 1943

My dearest—

The exam yesterday was an interesting ordeal to observe—more than a hundred men, all of whom have done some important things without a qualm, getting the freshman jitters. As the week went on, continuously the question was, "Do you think they'll ask this or that?" "What have you studied?" The excitement grew. I suppose everyone feels as I do, that I was the only one who remained calm, but there's no denying that each was to an extent affected by the collective emotion. We began at 8 A.M. and concluded at 5 P.M. with an hour for lunch. I was completely washed in physically at the end, but felt great mental relief, a descending calm.

Devotedly,
Colie

Clurie, Ann, and Carolyn, August 1, 1943.

Ann Harwell, Clurie, Carolyn, and Mayola, the Harwells' maid, drove to Charlottesville in late July. After a week's visit, the girls and Mayola went home by train. Ann stayed until Colie's departure August 16.

Ann to Colie

Charlottesville
Monday, August 16, 1943

My darling—

I thought when you left me today I couldn't bear it without at least a few more words with you. Such an unsatisfactory good-bye there at the roadside—so many things left unsaid.

I wonder if you realize how much I loved these three and a half weeks in Charlottesville. I shall cherish it always—this sweet house—which you were so wonderful to get—the beautiful days— people coming and going—the children—the lazy swims at the Club with you—hearing you enthuse over your German—watching you work—knowing you were close by and I could touch you—seeing you happy—having time to talk and laugh about little things together—Do you realize this is the first time in years that you've taken time to live like this? I love you so, darling—You're all I could ever ask for. But, God, don't be gone forever—Just the rest of this day since you left seems an eternity.

Oh, darling—let's finish this war—so we can get back to living again.

Take care of yourself—you're all life to me—none of it means anything without you.

Goodnight,
Ann

After Colie's departure, Ann drove home to Nashville, stopping overnight in Johnson City with the Allen Harrises. Although Colie was not permitted to tell Ann his location, his diary reveals that he had gone to Camp Patrick Henry, Virginia, before embarking for overseas assignment.

CHAPTER THREE

Moving On

Ann to Colie

Nashville
Friday, August 20, 1943

Colie, dearest—

The trip home was interminable—The first morning I went thirty-two miles off the proper road—when I realized what I'd done I just stopped the car and had a good cry. However, envisioned objectively it was a satisfactory trip—no car trouble—the gas held out well—although our quota in Tennessee has been dropped to three instead of four gallons. The Harrises were kind and patient—Then, of course, it was heaven to get home last night—my own house, my own people. I was exhausted in body and spirit—this business has been more of a shock than I had anticipated.

The children are fine. They are both enjoying their Army caps—Clurie has worn hers all day. Spent some time with Grandpa this afternoon. Marie and Josephine were over this morning—Jane, Rob, and children last night. I've been hiding out today. This war

Clurie, Ann Harwell, and Anne McLemore.

necessitates lots of guts—and every now and then they need relining—that's what I've been concentrating on today.

Devotedly,
Ann

Colie to Ann

Camp Patrick Henry
Sunday, August 22, 1943

My dearest—

Sunday rolls around like another day but there were the Sunday papers and church to remind of another world, of home and you, the children, and reality. This is definitely make believe, a transition between realities.

I went to 9:00 service in a pretty white chapel (the only painted building here). The service was good, the singing impressive—The eager nostalgic look in the boys' faces showed best what life is about.

After chapel, armed with a scrub brush and Octagon [soap], I trimmed down to shorts and joined the latrine rally. Now I have on the line my green zoot suit, towel, socks, underwear, and handkerchief. Someone aptly remarked that I look like a human Val-Pak [zip-up travel bag].

Now I'm sitting in the sun. Ed King has been writing also and Harry Lockeland is getting ready to sun in shorts and read. A bridge game goes on behind me on an improvised table in the edge of the woods. Sam Blair is sunning too. He is the contingent's conversationalist, especially at midnight, and if no one converses with him, he talks loudly to himself. The conversation is as funny and better to go to sleep on than the neighbor's radio. If you think I'm a ready

"Someone aptly remarked that I look like a human Val-Pak."

sleeper, you should see these guys—they drop off with screen doors slamming constantly, with unshaded lights two feet straight before them. No one expects quiet, they just crawl in their bunks and drop off.

And so goes the unreality, waiting for the day when I'm with you again. Moments come when it doesn't seem possible to be away from your hand and voice another day, then I fight to recall that this is not a day and time, but life's intermission.

Devotedly,
Colie

Colie to Ann

Camp Patrick Henry
Monday, August 23, 1943

My dearest—

Continuously there has been with me the memory of you. I cannot allow myself to think too much of you there in the home we love, the garden we love, the orchard we love—with our dear children—with you so very real yet beyond hearing or touching; so I must bring you away from it, to be here with me, to enjoy the idleness, the simple chores, the amusing instances, the cool morning air and the sun slanting through the tall trees. Whatever I do, you will share it, for I must have you always. We've had great joy together, haven't we? And fun, too, and deep satisfaction. In every moment of life I love you and adore you.

Forever,
Colie

Ann to Colie

Nashville
Monday, August 23, 1943

Darling—

Your letters arrived this morning. Let me know if I shall read parts of them to the family—I'm so busy keeping my mouth shut I wonder if I'm leaning too far backwards. I can't imagine you washing your own clothes—you see now why every housewife wants a Bendix [washing machine].

Your family has been superb about rallying around. Grandpa went so far as to say the drive home alone was too much for me to undertake—usually I have the feeling that he believes women have an endless capacity for any and all physical undertakings. We had dinner with them yesterday. Saturday night Sam and Jo took me to the Club with them for dinner—I'm very grateful for them—they're wonderful in-laws.

I'm terribly proud of you, darling—and proud that you want to do your part. Though none of that logic allays the loneliness—I shall go through the hours and the days, but in my heart I shall be living only for the time when we'll be together again.

Ann

Carolyn and Clurie with Sam Harwell Sr.

Colie to Clurie and Carolyn

Camp Patrick Henry
Tuesday, August 24, 1943

My darling girls—

The nicest part of my whole summer was during our days together in the house on Lewis Mountain Road. We had fun together, didn't we? Going to Buddy's for Coca-Colas, swimming at Farmington, and you playing while Mummy read and I studied. I hope it won't be so very long until we can all be together again.

In this camp, we live in big barracks made of wood, covered with black tar paper. Four of us stay in a small room, two sleeping in upper beds, two in the lower ones. I share one with Maj. Desmond, Maj. Levit, and Capt. Cavenaugh. When we get together in it, with all our equipment, we make a room full.

Things are planned very carefully in the army and each man carries whatever he may need. I wear high, laced shoes with thick leather and rubber soles; laced up leggins; regular khaki trousers tucked in the leggins; open necked shirt (soldiers don't wear ties in the field) and a helmet in two pieces. The underpiece has adjustable bands so that each man may fix it to fit. The outer part is steel and fits over the inner part neatly.

"I wear high, laced shoes with thick leather and rubber soles."

I wear a belt-suspenders arrangement to which my other equipment is attached. On the belt, over my left pocket, is a canteen which fits into a drinking cup and which swings in a canvas case. Over my right leg is a case for bullets, and in the middle of the belt at back is a medical kit. A field bag (called a musette bag) is attached to the suspenders in the rear and rests on my back. In it are clothes treated with chemicals to keep gas from hurting you. Also it carries an eating dish made in two pieces that are held together by a folding handle— and inside these are my knife, fork, and spoon. My raincoat also fits in the field bag. Then there is my blanket roll—two woolen blankets, half a tent (called a shelter half); one tentpole and pegs to hold it in

"A field bag is attached to the suspenders in the rear and rests on my back."

the ground are rolled up in a neat pack and tied around the musette bag. Under my left arm is my gas mask.

We eat in a big "mess hall," officers eating on one side and enlisted men on the other. In camp we don't use our individual mess kits, but the enlisted men do. Afterwards each soldier rinses his utensils in hot water and soap suds, then in two more barrels of clear hot water. They must keep their things very clean—otherwise they might get sick. The officers are served on aluminum trays with partitions in them. We carry our trays in the serving line and everything is put on the tray at the same time. They give us good things to eat and plenty of them. I expect I have gained weight since I came here.

I love you both very much.

Your devoted,
Daddy

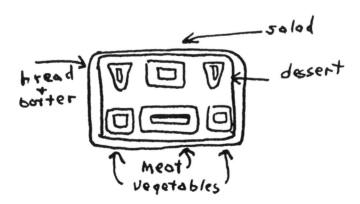

"The officers are served on aluminum trays with partitions in them."

Colie to Ann

Camp Patrick Henry
Wednesday, August 25, 1943

My dearest—

Your good letter, the first from home, arrived yesterday. I do hope being home makes things better for you. Keep busy with things, but not too busy—think of me, but do not worry—this is a great experience for which I wouldn't take anything—and you share every moment of it.

Your devoted husband,
Colie

Ann to Colie

Nashville
Wednesday, August 25, 1943

Darling—

It isn't possible, darling—that you are really so inaccessible. The days and particularly the nights lag so. I love you and need you so much. But I thank God too for the very fact of that need. Life would be dreadfully empty without that. Even though my heart is heavy— I'd rather have the burden of that love, that loneliness.

Devotedly,
Ann

On August 27, 1943, Coleman Harwell left Camp Patrick Henry and embarked by ship for North Africa.

Passage

Colie to Ann

Aboard ship
August/September, 1943

My Dearest—

I understand censorship permits us to say we are on a ship and well protected. The trip has its amount of monotony but also plenty of drama and beauty—the scene by day or night is so rare you want to ask what the name of the movie is.

Devotedly,
Colie

Ann to Colie

Nashville
Tuesday, August 31, 1943

Darling—

All the family, particularly the Howell contingent, are excited over Mortie's wedding to Nancy Watkins in St. Louis on September 25th. Marie is rooming us all at the hotel there as her treat. I'm going down this morning to see about a present—you and I and the Robert Harwells are giving something together—

silver, of course. Mortie is going to wear "whites" for the affair.

Last night Mother and I put up twelve quarts of tomatoes—they are beautiful. We have twenty-eight quarts of tomatoes, twenty-five quarts of string beans, twenty pints of applesauce, eleven pints of lima beans, peach preserves, canned blackberries, grape jelly—in addition to canned food I have bought—and a large amount of jelly and preserves left from last year. I believe we'll be in pretty good shape.

I had Jane and Rob, Barbara Jane Ketcham, and Louise Bray for Sunday dinner. The children ate with us and it was positively ludicrous to see Rob at table with seven females.

You're always on my mind and heart—

Devotedly,
Ann

On September 3, 1943, the British Eighth Army landed in Calabria in southernmost Italy, beginning the invasion of the Italian mainland.

Ann to Colie

Nashville
Friday, September 3, 1943

Darling—

Everyone is excited this morning over the news of the push against Italy itself. I'm wondering if you have heard of it and what bearing it will have on your personal plans.

Lena Dale initiated Julia, Dibbie, Val, and me into the mysteries of buying at the Classification Center grocery yesterday. We had a wonderful time—my excitement being over large Hershey bars— I've been mincing on them ever since.

Devotedly,
Ann

Colie to Ann

Aboard ship
September, 1943

My dearest—

These weeks since we parted have been years—into them has been crowded so much excitement, so much boredom, so much triviality embroidered into dramatics, and so much deep drama passing as trivia, all with God's beauty unsurpassed.

I have slept on sheets only twice since Charlottesville, recent nights I have slept in the open. I have been interested in taking a private course in astronomy from Don Roberts, who has a store of knowledge on mathematical and engineering subjects. Carl Eardley is our group leader—all of us have done some interesting things in this respect, planning, organizing for emergencies, etc. Last night gives a good slant on our way of life these days—Carl had his 38th birthday and we put on a gala at our supper. Our typed menu (which is fantastic considering our way of life) I fixed up in prep school humor—Italianesque style (with the aid of a corporal who used to be with UP [United Press] in Rome); Harry Haller mocked an embroidered towel with his sewing kit; I executed a few Houdinis and came up with an amazingly pleasant secret cocktail which was poured promptly at 4:50—supper being at 5:00. Lukens came through with a toast with such magnificence that he was still talking when the cocktails were going strong—which gives you an idea of how easy we are to entertain, or how eager we are for entertainment these days.

Last week Lukens and I discussed the possibility of having a church service with the enlisted men whose only officers are young lieutenants. It wound up with us holding the service. We realized that if we didn't hold it, it wouldn't be held, and since we were both officers in our churches (even though deacons and trustees are strictly dollar watchers) we felt it up to us. A number of the men attended. It was a dramatic scene outdoors and the officers said it went well— Lukens opened with a reading, Capt. Arthur Reede led the singing, I read a poem, the 23rd Psalm, and also a brief prayer, concluding with the Lord's prayer. Lukens wound up with a splendid short talk.

I introduced him by referring to the fact he'd seen all this before in the last war and has a nineteen-year-old son serving this time; he spoke very directly and sincerely of faith in God as the source of courage.

I wish I could give you a full picture of this life. Keeping cool is out of the question except outdoors; keeping clean is out of the question anywhere. There are three main compensations—we have enough to do to keep busy part of each day, recreation is pretty good with good companions, a sense of humor does many tricks. And the food is remarkably good. A lie detector would show I'm enjoying myself. My chief chore is putting out the daily typed news bulletin on top, headline news.

At night many of us sleep in the open, under the most beautiful sky you ever saw—I think of you most then as I look up at the stars. They are not part of this world, but they are bright reminders of the reality that lies behind and ahead with you at my side. God bless you and the girls, all the dear ones.

Devotedly,
Colie

Ann to Colie

Nashville
Sunday, September 5, 1943

Darling—

This morning Mother and I went to church. Bill preached the finest sermon I've ever heard—taking his text from how God limited Noah to the ark—and went on to show that although many of our lives are limited by illness, etc., the very fact of their being limited enables us to develop more by concentration, supplication, consecration.

After expecting to spend a rather empty Labor Day weekend, things are opening up. The Lindenberg girls decided to stir up something for tonight—so we are going to the Club for dinner—dutch. Tomorrow night Sam and Jo are having a dinner for some visiting Englishmen—and Tuesday night I'm going to the Sloans'.

I'm about to get the furnace in good shape. I hope it will be less temperamental than it was last year.

The girls are stirring—getting ready for a birthday party for the dolls. The tables are set up on the porch. Clurie has just come in with your cap on her head, a play gun strapped around her waist, and your old briefcase tied on her back like a pack—saying, "Reporting for duty, sir."

Devotedly,
Ann

Colie to Ann

Aboard ship
Sunday, September 5, 1943

My dearest—

It is Sunday night after a busy day. Lukens put me on the spot as I had put him last Sunday and insisted that I talk to the men this morning. We had a big turnout and it was a dramatic sight—men in undershirts, some not too well shaven, but with eager faces, gathered about. Lukens read from the sermon on the mount, Capt. Reede led hymns, Capt. Scott sang the "Holy City" as a solo. I read from Mark 5:13–16—"Ye are the salt of the earth—let your light so shine," and talked about their responsibility to remember home and what they stood for there.

I miss the company of Bill Levit, but believe it won't be long until we'll be together again. We have some good company, most of whom I believe you don't know. Dick Loeb is a bright fellow who went to Oxford after Yale, batted about Europe a good deal; Lockwood Thompson, a quiet, scholarly sort of fellow in Newton D. Baker's law firm in Cleveland; Charlie Phelps, a sturdy, quiet fellow from Buffalo; Hubert Stone, finance man from Connecticut; Geo. Geyer, California school man who lived at Miss Lewis's; Shirley Marsh, asst. attorney general of the state of Washington, and of course Carl, Ed, and Luke. Luke is a good Gibraltar—he is reading across the room and humming out of tune after making himself a sandwich that would shame Dagwood. A poker game goes on in the corner— Ecker-Racz, Don, and Haller have gone outside to see whether it's too inclement to sleep out.

These are long days and long nights without you, but I have happy memories to live on through many, many more.

Devotedly,
Colie

Colie to Clurie and Carolyn

Aboard ship
Wednesday, September 8, 1943

My darling girls—

I am having an interesting time traveling on this boat. Sometimes I sleep on the upper deck, sometimes on a canvas shelf that is in a big room of shelves four deep. We have good food but only eat twice a day—breakfast at 8:30 and supper at 5:00. In between I eat an apple or orange, cookies, or Coca-Cola. At night we have a plate of meat and cold cuts or cereal before going to bed. There are two kittens aboard, one gray and one black and white. They play all day and have a grand time. The ocean is beautiful—blue or green, depending on the sunlight, with foamy white caps everywhere. I make my own bed and wash my clothes, which I don't mind. I know you are both being good and helping every way you can.

Devotedly,
Daddy

On September 8, Allied forces announced that Italy had surrendered.

Colie to Ann

Aboard ship
Wednesday, September 8, 1943

My dearest—

At supper, the steward came down to shout, "Italy has surrendered unconditionally!" You can imagine the cheers that went up—I thought of you and wondered when you would hear the news.

Devotedly,
Colie

On Tuesday, September 7, 1943, Coleman A. Harwell II was born to Rob and Jane Harwell.

Ann to Colie

Nashville
Wednesday, September 8, 1943

Darling—

We had a Junior League membership meeting this morning—and just as Sara Mac was about to adjourn the meeting, someone whispered something to her. She held up her hand and then said, "Italy has surrendered to the Allies." It was such wonderful news—to think the war may be just a little shorter—and to think principally of the lives saved. Now to get the Germans out of Italy—and go on with the job.

Who do you suppose arrived yesterday morning at 9:45? Coleman A. Harwell II. He's a precious little baby with red hair. I spent about an hour with Jane this afternoon—she's fine.

The children send all kinds of love—I wish I could give you mine personally—how lovely that would be.

Devotedly,
Ann

Silliman Evans, publisher of the *Tennessean*, showed great concern for Colie and his family during the war.

Ann to Colie

Nashville
Friday, September 10, 1943

Darling—

Mr. Evans has crashed through! He saw Sam at the Club the other day and told him he had a check for you. Sam called me last night to tell me the check had arrived—guess how much—$1000—

Isn't that marvelous! Mother in her usual skeptical way said it was no more than he should have done.

All my love,
Ann

Colie to Ann

Aboard ship
Sunday, September 12, 1943

My dearest—

I have gone to sleep each night thinking of home—you in all my thoughts, the children, all the family—the garden, autumn flowers, the car, furnace, scores of small details—watching through the bathroom window as Clurie and Ellen run for the school bus, running toward one another, hair in the wind, shouting things the other never hears; Carolyn watching me shave, attentive as I splash water over

Clurie and Ellen Wills.

my face; breakfast in your bright, friendly little room; the car newly washed, delivered by Mitch and Will.

This morning we held another service and got George Geyer to make the talk. He did it excellently and I think it was really a fine service—I said the prayer, Lukens was emcee, Reede led the singing, Capt. Scott sang a nice solo, the finale was a splendid tenor solo by an Irish youngster—Waters's "Ave Maria."

Devotedly,
Colie

Ann to Colie

Nashville
Sunday, September 12, 1943

My darling—

You seem so close today—I felt that you were with me in church—I thought of that last sunlit Sunday in Charlottesville— every moment will be engraved on my heart and mind—even the picture of me standing over the ironing board in my best clothes pressing your shirt. More and more I find life's real meaning hidden in little things—the things that make you laugh and the things that make you cry because they are so precious.

I don't believe I would change anything in our life together— Even this war, this dreadful separation must be borne—because it's part of the balanced picture—but how hard it is—particularly today—you've seemed so close and yet so unattainable—my mind has been holding my heart in check—but somehow today the formula just won't work.

Ann

CHAPTER FIVE

North Africa
Training Continues

*I*n September Coleman Harwell arrived in North Africa.

Ann to Colie

Nashville
Thursday, September 16, 1943

Darling—

Mother took Clurie in town this afternoon to see a Henry Aldrich movie—then Carolyn and I went in on the bus at 4:45 and met them for dinner. We went to Kleeman's where you can get a pot roast dinner with all the fixings from soup through salad and dessert for 75¢—then came out on the 7:00 bus. With our gas quota cut and my B book [ration book] not yet renewed, I'm finding it advisable to use the bus more and more.

We are getting ready to go to the wedding. After telling Marie I couldn't buy a dress and go too, I went ahead and bought one. Marie has completely loosened the purse strings with a regular trousseau for herself from Weinberger's. It should be a good show.

Devotedly,
Ann

Colie to Ann
[Near Casablanca] North Africa
Friday, September 17, 1943

My dearest—

If you are picturing me in charge of a city somewhere, you're wrong for the first time in your life—I am commander of a platoon of troops in a temporary camp, for the time being. It is a training camp, for us as well as the men. After this we should know the army. Today I was in charge of fifty men remaking the parade ground. And such work—hauling rock, filling big gaps, grading—just the thing a newspaper editor is best suited to. Seriously, it does require use of your head to handle that many men, to deal with officers, and to get things done to the satisfaction of the camp commander.

We have set up an organization from the ground up—tents with wooden slat beds, we have established our own messes, and all the customary inspection, policing, etc., officers, and non-com set up. It is interesting to see what ingenuity can do with tin cans, scrap lumber, pots and pans scraped up by our battalion supply officer. And to hear Ecker-Racz (once the pride of Morgenthau [Henry Morgenthau Jr. was Secretary of the Treasury from 1934–1945], now the prided mess officer of our company) explain how cranberry juice was made potable by adding lemon juice.

Our food has been adequate, but none too fancy. For a time we had salmon and spam, spam and salmon twice a day, and hash for breakfast. But today we had real scrambled eggs, oatmeal without milk, bread, butter, and almost coffee for breakfast; a piece of very edible beef, mashed potatoes, fruit for lunch; salmon, potatoes, a tomato each, delicious half of a Bermuda onion, apple butter, bread and cranberry juice. That gives you a good idea of how the army works to keep the diet rounded.

Devotedly,
Colie

Ann to Colie

Nashville
Saturday, September 18, 1943

Darling—

Yesterday morning I got your cable that you had arrived. Western Union woke me up with the message. I called Sam and woke him up—Rob was already up. Clurie was excited and wanted to know if it meant you had gotten where you were going. Carolyn wanted to know if you were coming home. Archie however takes the cake— Mother beat me to it and told him first—you know her faculty for that. I could hear her telling him downstairs, and I could hear Archie say something to the effect that he certainly was glad because he didn't think I could have stood it much longer. Then when I came downstairs he said, "Mrs. Harwell, I'm just as glad as you are." He's taking this whole war very seriously and, having been in the last one, he feels that he speaks with great authority.

I thank the good Lord that you are on land—even though I don't know where. Do take care of yourself.

Devotedly,
Ann

Ann to Colie

Nashville
Monday, September 20, 1943

Darling—

Picked up Hank Fort [Eleanor Hankins Fort] today and brought her out from town. She wanted to know where you were and when I said I didn't know, she said—"Well, I bet wherever he is, he's running things." So you see you have a large and appreciative audience. Not the least of whom is your own little wife.

Devotedly,
Ann

Colie left Casablanca by train on September 21.

Colie to Ann

Aboard train, North Africa
Wednesday, September 22, 1943

My dearest—

We are en route by train to another location. Our experience in battalion and company organization was invaluable, our command of troops gave us a confidence that can stand us in good stead if circumstance later should throw us into command positions.

Our food continues to improve. We had the same as the men, served in an officers' mess at slab tables. We had pancakes, fresh eggs, frozen beef a couple of times, canned peas and spinach as delicious as you've ever tasted; either butter or peanut butter, chili, frankfurters and kraut, and many good sweet things like apple butter, pitted cherries, mixed fruit.

There was a P-X at the camp, with a good stock of toilet articles, a limited but good stock of candy, Old Golds, Philip Morris, and Pall Mall cigarettes, and a few other items. Ration cards are issued on these things—for instance, you are allowed four cartons of cigarettes a month at 45¢ a carton; two bars of delicious, tropical Hersheys; four packs of gum, eight of Lifesavers, and other sweet items such as a small box of gum drops. I also bought my four bars of soap and four packages of razor blades.

I was much interested in reading my men's mail—it is censored by a unit officer, then by a base censor. The boys were from all over—Brooklyn, New Jersey, Iowa, Nebraska, Alabama. With a few exceptions, they were amazingly illiterate, and I'm sure many had never written letters before. They generally were of the "I don't have nothing to do today, so will write you. . . . there ain't much news, so I will now close." There were practically no complaints, nearly every one was filled with messages to relatives and friends and asking questions about events at home; several were married with babies. Many were to brothers also in the service in far places and often not heard from in months. All were eager for news from home and one said he'd reread his old letters so many times he'd practically memorized them. One of the boys made a cute remark about his officer. "It's pretty hard on him," he said, "having to read all those homesick letters when he's probably homesick too." He spoke a mouthful.

There was adequate recreation for both men and officers. The Red Cross had a day room in camp and places where the men could get chocolate and sandwiches or cookies at night—there was also a recreation center where the men could buy limited amounts of beer and wine. And a large Red Cross center in town. For the officers there was a beautiful club, simple but attractive in white stucco tropical style. There was a long bar, where a poor beer and native wine were sold. The wine was not too bad, but a bit too sweet and with a strange kick if you didn't watch it, so I did. I am still carrying my quart of rum and two pints of bourbon and have tasted hard liquor only once since Charlottesville, when Dick Loeb broke out a pint of fifteen-year-old bourbon for eighteen of us to celebrate the surrender of Italy with a sip each.

One day at our first camp in Africa, Ed Smith, Dick Loeb, and I got passes and went to town together. Dick speaks fluent French, and that was a help. We went first to an army P-X where he was trying to buy a watch. Then, at nearly 2:00, we found a restaurant. It was of the sidewalk type, typically French, a little dirty but passable. Its chief recommendations were the people there—a handsome young French officer and a pretty girl, a group of well tailored businessmen, two family groups with children. One little girl, Clurie's age, was dropping bread under the table to a fancily-trimmed French poodle. We took a table on the sidewalk and immediately the expected happened—a swarm of Arab children began beseeching us for money and food. Unfortunately you can't give one anything for that would bring them in droves from all the area, so we had to ignore even the one who did acrobatics. We had good hors d'oeuvres—quartered tomatoes, the only fresh ones I've tasted this year besides the wonders you brought to Charlottesville; tasty lentils with onions; a good cold bean dish. Our main course was a reintroduction to meat, a delicious veal cutlet. We had two glasses apiece of beer, none too good, but clean tasting and ice cold. For dessert we could not resist fresh grapes, as good as they looked. The price for everything was about 30 francs, or 60¢ each.

After lunch we saw the city. It has many handsome modern buildings—banks, hotels, apartments, and homes. There are several big department stores in addition to numerous shops. Leather goods are featured in many, but prices have gone sky high and I saw nothing worthwhile beyond a few small wallets. We did most of our looking in the largest store which has quite a continental atmosphere if a scanty supply. We saw some rayon hose and apparently there was a good supply of women's wear—but all clothing staples are rationed. The food department had only caviar and other fancy fare, native wine and a reputedly poor native scotch which we ignored. I noticed that the luggage supply included unfinished calf suitcases for 2,000 francs—about $40—and others made of wood. I was interested in the wooden homemade-looking toys cruder than toycrafter efforts.

The only major attraction remaining was the movie theater. It was in a cleft cut in the red soil where apparently there had been a rock quarry. Its seating capacity about equaled Nashville's East High stadium and its free attractions drew capacity audiences every night. I saw two very good films—*Hello Frisco* with Alice Faye, and Jimmy Cagney in the Canadian flying movie [*Captains of the Clouds*, filmed in 1940]. This, too, was a dramatic scene under the open skies—with an occasional plane overhead, an occasional searchlight in the sky.

The campsite at first gave the appearance of barrenness—but it was at various levels in rolling country and especially at dawn or twilight was a trim, attractive scene. Around it were constant streams of Arabs—with small camel caravans, in groups or singly riding their tiny donkeys. A few of them were allowed admittance to the camp, a shine boy and some laundry men. I let one of the Arabs take my dirty clothes. He brought them back in twenty-four hours, smelling of chlorine, sandy in color. They're better than they were, but I'm hoping to find good facilities somewhere ahead.

The Arabs have learned many English expressions, most of them vulgar but expressive, in the best G-I manner—G-I (general issue) is used to apply to everything, including the enlisted man, who has become a G-I in this war, just as he was a doughboy in the last.

I believe you can see this is a tremendously interesting experience—I scarcely miss creature comforts, but constantly my heart and thoughts are with you and home—Hug my dear girls, give my love to all—remember you are in my heart every minute—

Devotedly,
Colie

CHAPTER SIX

North Africa Letters from Afar

Ann to Colie

Nashville
Monday, September 27, 1943

Darling, darling—

The time has come when I refuse to pretend that I don't need you. I realize now that I need you every minute of the day and night—I'm competent to get things done—I am even managing to pretend the light touch—I'm getting quite facile about many things—but under the veneer I need you as I never have before. There will never be any real peace, any real joy until we are together again.

Your trip over must have been like something dreamed up in a book. I found your passages about the services particularly appealing. How strange it must have seemed to you—in the middle of the ocean—cut off from everything—I should think there would have been a certain peace there that could not be found in a church—because you really had placed yourselves in the hands of God.

Mortie and Nancy's wedding was very pretty. We had quite a delegation on the train—Marie, Mort, Mortie, Martha Bartles, Leila, Josephine, myself, and Mrs. Hooper Love. Mort called us his

Nancy and Morton Howell Jr. at their wedding, September 25, 1943.

musical comedy troop—and we made enough noise for that. Later Louise and Clopper Almon and Frances Ewing and son Bob arrived. Marie put us up in great style at a beautiful hotel. The Watkinses' connections entertained us royally and I actually managed to come home a few pounds heavier.

Devotedly,
Ann

Colie to Ann

North Africa
Sunday, October 3, 1943

My dearest—

Yesterday we went into the nearby city and had a delightful day— its boulevards are like Paris; many handsome shops (with bare shelves); great, modern apartment buildings and hotels. But all very crowded. Saw several people I knew, including Don Whitehead of the AP [Associated Press]. Missed Whitaker who is now a Lt. Col. The trip (by truck) is through some of the most beautiful country imaginable. Worst disappointment is there's nothing left to buy but junk at unbelievable prices.

Devotedly,
Colie

Ann to Colie

Nashville
Tuesday, October 5, 1943

Darling—

I'm constantly grateful for your magnificent zest for living—it will carry you over many rough spots—as I can see it has already. I'm proud of you, proud to be able to say my husband is overseas, proud to wear the little service pin with its one star. You're marvelous and I adore you—

Ann

Ann to Colie

Nashville
Thursday, October 7, 1943

Darling—

You'd never guess what I'm doing on Monday nights! Con has dug up two South Americans and they are teaching us Spanish. Eight of us, including Julia Fay, Val, and Dakie, sat in the Thompson living room and concentrated like mad for two hours. My mind creaks noticeably and I could wish it were Italian or German, but it is an opportunity and I believe will be a help.

I wish I could send you some flowers out of the garden—the coloring is brilliant—yellows, pinks, and reds. The Meadows have a flock of turkeys—and Mother is fretting because she didn't raise a few. I'm terribly afraid we're going to have chickens yet.

Take care of yourself—and know how much we love you—

Ann

Colie to Ann

North Africa
Saturday, October 9, 1943

My dearest—

Last night I hit the jackpot when our mail clerk laid down six letters from you. The big news was the arrival of the baby and that Janie is fine. The thought of the three boys, in almost exactly the same steps as we were, is of a picture I couldn't want changed. I'm tremendously pleased that they named him for me—brothers and sisters sometimes are not so close that their children grow into such devotion; I feel that our children are fortunate to be close to uncles and aunts and cousins. And—though mine is a pretty heavy name to wish off on a fellow—I like the idea of a Sam, Robert, and Coleman in another generation. I never cease to thank God for our glorious children—yours and mine—Ann and Carolyn always are and will be in my heart where no one can be but you. For them now I am especially happy that another cousin adds to an already wonderful family circle.

Devotedly,
Colie

Colie to Ann

North Africa
Sunday, October 10, 1943

My dearest—

I spent the early morning hours today at personal chores, getting out laundry to be poorly but somewhat cleanly done; sorting out my belongings including an extra blouse [coat], winter underwear, wool shirts and trousers, and some other odds and ends I was able to get in the nearby city; priding myself on a good supply of such essentials as razor blades and other toiletries; also have a luxurious chewing gum supply and several cartons of cigarettes.

After noon, I walked into the village. The contrast between clean, orderly civilization and the Arab life of filth and flies is always shocking. The occasional appearance of a spotless Arab in white turban and cloak is even more surprising. And, too, the partial observance of Sunday—with Christians at church, at leisure; the Arabs about their chores, washing without soap, jogging about on their little jackasses; shoveling manure up next to their houses. I find the young and middle-aged natives unappealing—the little ones and the very old, however, seem to be just people and they attract me. Some of the children are very good looking and their faces remarkably expressive. A little girl Clurie's age, with pure white skin and coal eyes and hair; a crowd gathered at a corner water pipe filling pots and pans for the day. Then the old ones—a gnarled, straggly-haired old woman with a scarf around her head, bare feet, sitting on the dirt sidewalk; an old man of great dignity, with curling beard and huge turban, trudging along on his cane, smiling and saying a gracious "bon jour." Another old geezer trying to mount his jackass—he almost gets into the unstirruped saddle, loses his balance and plops onto the ground, jabbering curses.

In the afternoon I accomplished a long delayed chore—cleaned the sand and dust from my gun, oiled it—was pleased with the job. So to an engagement with Don, Ed, and Haller for dinner at one of the little hotels here, and it resulted in a feast. We had drinks first— a peppery brandy, hardly passable at home, but all right here. Then the banquet: soup the first course; second, a slice of beef with spicy gravy and a dish of pea puree; third, roast chicken, very good and apparently cooked in olive oil; fried sweet potatoes; finally, dried figs and coffee. The bill was 135 francs [$2.70] each, but we didn't complain, as it was our week's extravagance. The dining room is simple, no tablecloths or napkins, but very clean, with a huge Frigidaire the chief furnishing of the room. The little French lady runs it from a glassed-in office and is very genteel and pleasant. The room was filled with officers, a few decidedly high class civilians, and one Arab—a middle-aged, handsome, white-turbaned gentleman, much of the Valentino air, who was said to be a chieftain.

By the way, I've been issued the North Africa theater service ribbon. I don't wear it here, since the fact is obvious and I'd like to do some more important things before being beribboned. I'd send it to you, but hesitate to trust it in the mail, so if you happen by Burk's, I feel sure you can buy one. You have the right to wear it and certainly you deserve to.

Devotedly,
Colie

Ann to Colie

Nashville
Monday, October 11, 1943

Darling—

Clurie, I, Ellen, Jesse, little Ellen, Ellen's father, Dr. Buckner, Florence Fletcher, and little Florence all went to the circus together. Jesse got the seats for us—which was a great help. The children had a wonderful time. Clurie particularly liked the clowns—and squealed with delight when the little house is set on fire and the clowns run to put it out. It seemed to me that they went principally to eat—they had Coca-Cola, cotton candy, ice cream, peanuts, and Dr. Buckner had brought along a bag of apples.

I looked out the back in the moonlight last night and felt that my heart would break if you didn't come home to me soon. I love you so much, darling—love you and think of you every minute.

Devotedly,
Ann

CHAPTER SEVEN

North Africa
The End of an Interlude

Colie to Ann

North Africa
Thursday, October 14, 1943

My dearest—

Tonight Don and I went to keep Harry company with a gin rummy game, as he was on duty. Walking home in the moonlight we heard eerie screeches, running like a chant or wail, and saw a bright fire burning in the Arab village. It apparently marked a feast occasion, perhaps a wedding. The Arabs are never-ending sources of wonderment—I should think missionary work among them would be the world's most futile job.

Devotedly,
Colie

Ann to Colie

Nashville
Sunday, October 17, 1943

My darling—

Becky Looney is in town, having come to see her brother Alex Porter, who is home on leave. She was talking of moving to

Oklahoma and how her husband, Bob, had the house full of flowers when they arrived and no food in the house for the baby—it suddenly came over me in a great wave what being without you meant to me— I had to leave the room—all the intimate details, details that would be unimportant to anyone but me—having you reach out your hand to me—a dozen little things—I try to carry on and for the most part I do a damn good job—even if I do say so myself—but this is one of those nights when it's almost too much for me. I try to realize that this is war and that I should be deeply grateful for living where I do with the same comforts, but tonight nothing makes sense except that you are away and that I have no idea when I'll see you.

Devotedly,

Ann

Colie to Ann

North Africa

Monday, October 18, 1943

My dearest—

Had the best bridge game I've indulged in yet last night with Clarke, Lewis, and Smith. Clarke is jolly as ever and highly pleased with himself. However, Smith and I took them to the sum of thirty francs each, which gives you an idea not only as to the height of the stakes but also as to how close the game was. I have played half a dozen times and enjoyed it a great deal, have even learned the Blackwood convention. By the time I get home, I should be able to play even with you.

I can't tell you how much I love you and miss you—I have a snapshot of the girls on the desk beside me—I can picture the beautiful flowers you have described in your letters—there never have been any flowers as pretty as the ones you raise. I'm so glad you are enjoying the house. I think of it many times, how very livable it is and how perfectly it suits our needs; how someday you will be able to do those things that need doing to make it perfect: a beautiful rug in the living room, the chair rail, and a pretty paper for the dining room.

I'm glad you are getting satisfaction from the Junior League work—certainly you could not be putting your fine talents to a greater public service—You got as fine a compliment as one could imagine when, in this faraway place, your friend Dr. Williams said, "Oh, yes, you are the husband (haven't you turned the tables, though!) of Mrs. Harwell of the Junior League." I said, "Yes, I am one of the husbands of one of the Harwells," and he said, "Oh, I know which one. She has been to see me often and is doing a splendid job with the Junior League Home. It is always a pleasure to work with her." He went to the head of my class immediately.

And your Spanish sounds very smart. Of course I feel nervous about all you *war widdies* and some South Americans, but even at that I'm in favor of it.

Adding to my good feeling tonight probably is the fact that I took a walk into the country this afternoon—through the town and out into some of the most glorious hill country you've ever seen—it was late and the road was busy with old broken down autos and donkey carts—with laden jackasses jogging along—one Arab had a brand new disk fresh from the blacksmith—this is market season and the countryside is busy—the prettiest sight of all was a lovely stucco bungalow on the edge of town, with trim garden terraces, a straw-hatted Arab hired man working away under directions of a trim woman in white gardening costume—it was more like you and Archie than anything I've seen.

I love you with all my heart, dearest. I love you and the girls, you and home, you and even this strange place, which doesn't seem half so strange tonight, because you seem very much a part of it, and I feel very much at ease.

Devotedly,
Colie

Ann to Colie

Nashville
Wednesday, October 20, 1943

Darling—

They are starting a Brownie scout troop at Parmer and Clurie went to her first meeting Monday. I was over at the school today to get our new ration books and one of the women there said—you are Ann Harwell's mother, aren't you. She was one of the scout leaders— well, she said, Ann was the first one to come to scouts and when she walked in the room she said—my name is Ann Harwell; my father is Captain Harwell—and I can tell where he is. So you see we not only are not forgetting you, but we continue to keep you very much in the forefront of our thoughts.

Kindergarten is doing a lot for Carolyn—She continues to demand quite a bit of service—makes Archie open and butter her bread every night—and fix her baked potato—of course he loves it.

Mother and Clurie are having their difficulties. Mother has to tell her how to do everything and the child will not take it. It's a rather difficult situation, because Mother feels badly about it—and I must make the child show the proper respect, and yet in my heart I know the child's point of view is the right one.

Mr. Evans has been eager for news of you—so I read him excerpts from some of your letters—I went to the office and had a nice visit with him. I took the liberty of telling him (though not in so many words) that you felt badly because you had not heard from him. He seemed rather startled. I believe he wrote you the next day. He called me himself a few days later to ask if I wanted some passes to the circus. I thanked him, but told him someone had already gotten mine. He insisted that I should call anytime I wanted tickets—said I should have a priority there.

Next morning

Tuesday I went to an auction sale at Cheekwood. It was held in the courtyard of the stable; you never saw such a turnout of people in your life—Belle Meade showed up in full force—Mrs. Cheek herself had a front row seat. They sold everything from lamps to Victorian vases and old wicker chairs. The prices were exorbitant— they even sold a swivel chair and desk which they said was Mr. Cheek's—Josephine said some man bought them because he could sit in the chair and dream of being a coffee millionaire.

I finally had a letter from our landlady in Charlottesville. She said: "I consider myself most fortunate to have had such obviously

Marie Howell, Rob Harwell, Josephine Harwell, Sam Harwell Jr., Jane Harwell, Barbara Jame Ketcham, Mort Howell Jr. at an evening party at the Belle Meade Country Club, December 23, 1941.

well bred people in my house. My mother let a colonel and his wife have her house while she was away and they left everything in simply disgusting condition." The light bill ran around $14, which seems exorbitant, the phone around $10—then she found a broken ashtray—so I sent her a check this morning to cover all three items.

The Blandfords are here visiting at Harding Place—there have been many parties for them and although it has kept me busy I've really enjoyed myself. It's nice to see people other than just those connected with my Junior League work.

Your family has been marvelous in making me feel that they are standing behind me. I don't know how I would get along without them—not that they do so much—though they do plenty—but it is the wonderful realization that I know they are there if the need should arise. Mother said Sam said the other night to Grandpa, "I want Ann to know that she has a man behind her."

Sammy returns home this weekend. He is being sent to the Classification Center—can you imagine better luck?

Same night

I took Clurie to see *This Is the Army* this afternoon—Mother and Carolyn came in later to meet us for dinner at Kleeman's.

We've had three Spanish lessons and have learned quite a lot. There is no fee—so to do my share I had Con and the professor to dinner last Monday—the children were enthralled—he was a delightful guest and of course had an unusual way of talking. The only difficulty is finding time to study in between. We are now working on the verbs—which is rather easy for me because it is much like Latin—I'm quite delighted to have some project that calls for the use of some gray matter.

I am getting the living room draperies you promised me for an anniversary present and am having the Knox sofa recovered— because more and more I feel the need of having people with me here in my own house. We invite people and tell them to bring their own liquor—it is almost a physical impossibility to buy any.

Devotedly,

Ann

Ann to Colie

Nashville

Sunday, October 24, 1943

Darling—

Bill Phifer wanted me to teach a Sunday School class of sixteen-year-old girls—I really was quite touched, but did not feel that I could obligate myself to such now—I'm not prepared for it and haven't the time to prepare myself now. Too many things to do get me frantic and present a definite mental hazard.

Do you have any idea how much I do need you? There are very few hours of the day when I don't wish for your sane counsel—but most of all just for you. If this war lasts for ten years, I'll still be waiting—needing you more each day.

All my love,
Ann

Colie to Clurie and Carolyn

North Africa
Monday, October 25, 1943

My darling girls—

Last night three other officers and I had dinner at the hotel in this town where I am staying. There was a pretty little baby at a table near ours and after dinner I told the mother and father that I liked babies because I had two pretty ones who are now pretty little girls. Then I showed them your pictures.

Most of the people who live in this country are Arabs. They live in houses made of mud with straw thatched roofs or tile. They ride little jackasses or camels around. Many have farms and on a market day such as last Saturday they ride one jackass and lead another one, and bring vegetables in to sell. They carry things in big straw bags that look like straw hats. The jackasses are gentle and stand still while their masters sell things out in the market place—just like the farmers at home bring things to the square in front of Grandpa's

"The other day I saw a fat Arab in a bright orange turban and cloak riding a tiny donkey."

store. The other day I saw a fat Arab in a bright orange turban and cloak riding a tiny donkey. He had a big stomach and looked very funny, but the donkey didn't seem to mind. They looked something like this. You will notice some flies flying around the donkey's head—the donkey is very patient and doesn't even seem to mind them.

The people here have a way of getting local news that has long since played out in our country since newspapers were started. They have a town crier. He walks all over town, tapping on a big drum and every now and then he stops at a corner and reads out something very fast in French. He wears a little beret and seems to take himself very seriously. This is the way he walks. The funny thing is, when he reads his news, nobody pays any attention, so sometimes he stands and just sputters it out all to himself. But he makes up for it by beating the drum so loudly the people have to listen.

"*They have a town crier. . . . This is the way he walks.*"

The Arabs don't have running water in their homes, but there is a water plug every now and then on a corner. The children bring buckets and big clay vases and fill them up for the day's supply. They are very busy about the job but sometimes they stop to play and their mothers come out and call to them in Arabic in words that mean, "Hurry up." And then they do hurry. This is something like the way it looks every morning. You can see the mother calling to the little girls to stop dancing and bring the water.

They have little farms on the mountain side and you will see goats eating grass or anything else right on the steepest slopes. There are olive trees, too, but the olives aren't good to eat until they've been pickled. The houses open onto a narrow, steep path. As we walked through the village we saw lots of people, some very old

"This is something like the way it looks every morning."

ones sitting in the sun and lots of little children playing. They smiled very pleasantly and all said "bon jour" to us. Many little children took out after us and asked for "bonbon, Johnnie" or "chew gum, Johnnie—thank you very much." They like candy and gum the Americans bring—they don't have any over here.

I am getting along fine and like the army, but I miss all of you a great deal. Clurie, I am very proud of how well you are doing in school and know you enjoy it. I'm glad you are going to kindergarten, Carolyn, and getting along fine. You are mighty smart big girls.

I am proud of you both and love you very much.

Devotedly,
Daddy

Ann to Colie

Nashville
Tuesday, October 26, 1943

Darling—

Halloween is this weekend—and I decided it was time Ann had a party—so we are having one Friday afternoon with about eighteen little girls attending. It's funny how you never get any refusal for a children's party—They are all coming in costume and we are going to bob for apples and have ice cream and cake and a treasure hunt with corn candy. Carolyn is as excited about the whole thing as though it were her own idea. She's very much interested in music now—has me play records and the piano for her continuously.

Devotedly,
Ann

Ann to Colie

Nashville
Thursday, October 28, 1943

Darling—

The cook asked me today if you would be home for Christmas— I wish you would—but we'll get through somehow—like Scarlett I just don't think about that.

Everything here goes well—the countryside beautiful—we are still getting a few tomatoes out of the garden—and a few roses now and then—Darling, how I miss you—I need you constantly—

All my love,
Ann

CHAPTER EIGHT

North Africa
Making a Change

On October 31, Colie was traveling by train across North Africa.

Colie to Ann

Aboard train, North Africa
Sunday, October 31, 1943

My dearest—

This is another beautiful Sunday morning—there is the unexpected white steeple of a church rising from a green copse—rich black soil freshly turned by eight-animal teams—the fields busy with farmer Arabs. The rugged hills are gray-brown, the lower lands changing from rocky gorges to gray wasteland to wide fields of black and brown—occasional hillside olive groves with beautiful silvery-green trees of every shape—in the distance great trees surrounding a farm home, nearby a strawstack secured by a mud-pack coating—passing a stucco rail station shaded by a beautiful eucalyptus tree—an auto along the smooth, winding oil highway—I woke up at 5:30 with a pain in my ribs, but expected that from sleeping in the baggage rack. But the pain was soon gone and Frank Brennan and I hopped out at the first stop, looking for native coffee. We were lucky—a native Red Cross canteen was open. There was coffee served in C ration [canned meals used to feed the U.S. armed forces] tins. Then there was a meat spread on a huge slice of brown bread and a grape jelly sandwich—This was supplemented by good yellow cheese generously scooped from his bucket by a British officer—and a native orange, one of a dozen we bought the night before.

Ed Smith is with me in the compartment, with Les Dawson, Brennan, and another man named Craig. To improve sleeping conditions, we divided—one to each seat below, one to each baggage rack—and hung shelter halves between the racks to make the fifth bunk.

Last night at a stop I observed the general scene of going to bed, one of the most comic sights ever. Every compartment seemed to be packed with men in all conditions of undress, men hanging from the wall, helmets, musette bags, shelter halves, canteens, cans, hung from top to bottom in amazing confusion, and apparently everybody was doing something—folding blankets, eating, undressing, or just pushing around being in the way. That's how it looked from trackside.

Devotedly,
Colie

Ann to Colie

Nashville
Sunday, October 31, 1943

Darling—

This has been one of those days that I could never have dreamed up in my wildest flights of fancy—and yet I have survived—the cook came up yesterday to say that her husband had arrived for a week's leave—so, of course, she left immediately. Today was Archie's Sunday off—I cooked breakfast—got the children off to Sunday School—cleaned the house—took Mother to church, brought the children back—finished cleaning—got myself and girls together in time to meet a friend of Dort Banner's and met Mother at the Club for dinner. Brought Dort's friend here afterwards—sat around between times—then walked to Grandpa's—had nice visit with him—walked home—arriving after 6:00—fixed supper with Clurie assisting—put two loads of clothes in the Bendix—while Mother washed the dishes, Clurie took a bath—and Carolyn rode merrily around the basement on their tricycle—then girls in bed about 8:30—hung up washing—made some phone calls—gave myself a bath—and here I am with the paper not even read yet. It's a great life—I tell you this not to worry you—but just to give you a glimpse of "my day."

Ann

Ann to Colie

Nashville
Monday, November 1, 1943

Darling—

We are in the middle of another coal strike—I don't know how they will work this one out.

The Halloween party was cute—they all wore costumes—and were a sight all out in the yard running around. A man and woman and a soldier came by while they were in the yard and asked to take their pictures—the man had a roll of colored film and said if the pictures were any good he would send me one.

Last night after I had finally settled back against the pillows at 10:40 to read the paper the phone rang—and to make a long story short—I had to get out of bed, dress, get out the car, and go get Blackout at the Percy Warner Apartments. The phone rang while I was writing this and I have had to go after him again. It was funny last night—but I'm mad today and am going to call Rob tomorrow and see if he knows anyone who would like to have him. I'm very fond of him in a way, but he is turning into a miserable pest. He tries to get on the school bus—so we have to tie him up every morning before Clurie goes to school.

Halloween party.

I'm very proud of your service ribbon—makes the whole thing sound distinctly authentic—no more giggles from me, my friend, when someone salutes you.

Devotedly,

Ann

By November 1, Colie had arrived in Bizerte. On November 4, he and his fellow officers left Bizerte and North Africa, bound for Sicily.

Ann to Colie

Nashville

Thursday, November 4, 1943

Darling—

The coal strike has finally been settled with Ickes [Harold Ickes, Secretary of the Interior] doing the bargaining instead of the WLB [War Labor Board]—though I believe the latter has to approve the agreement. I'm grateful it has been cleared. There are many things about the domestic scene I should like to talk to you about—but hesitate to do so in a letter. The Moscow conference sounded thrilling, and one feels that Hull has made an outstanding contribution—I'm sure too that [Anthony] Eden must be a remarkable person. I am of course delighted with even the smallest gains made in Italy—if only they could do the job quickly and save some lives—I hate to think of the devastation.

Tonight was the yearly spaghetti dinner at Parmer School—so the four of us dressed up and went. The food was very good—and everybody was there.

Carolyn fell down Sunday and sprained her ankle. Nothing serious—but we have been keeping her off her feet and applying packs—we are letting her walk a little now though we still carry her most places—which is rather a chore. Mother got the old cart out of the attic and Ellen, Clurie, and Mannie Jackson wheel her out each afternoon. This afternoon they went over to the Hales' and spent about an hour playing with Nancy.

They are starting the first Gray Lady class at the new hospital here and I was fortunate enough to be one of those selected—I say fortunate because confidentially I believe there were a lot who wanted to do it. I've been anxious to do something that would be a direct contribution to the soldier—as much as anything because you are a soldier—and I want to do my bit. The course itself will probably take more time than I have to give, but after it is over—I will be expected to give only one day a week—and I can manage that. So I'm quite happy about it.

I love you every minute.

Ann

CHAPTER NINE

Sicily

On November 4, Colie arrived in Palermo, Sicily.

Colie to Ann

Sicily
Sunday, November 7, 1943

My dearest—

I have just finished a marvelous Red Cross charabanc tour of some beautiful and amazing scenes of Sicilian history. I am billeted in what was a beautiful apartment with oil painted ceiling in one room, gilt decorated ceiling in my room, two baths, and kitchen. The come-down is there are two men to a room with Army cot and chair for each as furniture and the strictly cold water runs a short time twice a day.

I have a British roommate, a very nice middle-aged gent—We have a batman named Chesworth and a janitor named Salvatore who acts like all four Marx brothers at once.

I was at our headquarters when a familiar voice greeted me—it was Alden, just dropped by to see if I was in the neighborhood. He had lunch with us and we swapped experiences which just about covers this part of the world by air and ground.

All my love,
Colie

Ann to Colie

Nashville
Friday, November 12, 1943

Darling—

There is almost nothing to be found here in the way of toys—almost everything is made of paper. I have ordered two WAC [Women's Army Corps] outfits from New York. Mother has bought two dolls—and we have had trouble finding any thin material with which to make clothes for them. People are buying frantically, but the quality of the merchandise in the stores is dreadful.

I'm deep in the Gray Lady course—three times a week until the first of December.

It appears to me that there is less and less time that I can call my own—always demands from others and so little that can be really mine—perhaps if you were here and we had a life together I wouldn't feel it all so strongly.

Devotedly,
Ann

Colie to Ann

Sicily
Sunday, November 14, 1943

My dearest—

Dr. Williams took Ed, Halley, and me in his big Fiat to the beautiful cathedral here for high Mass this morning. It was beautiful in the twilight and the drive was magnificent. A comic touch was added by having to push the car and as we started back, when a swarm of kids joined in the push, most of them riding and I think a few holding it back.

I've spent recent days thinking of you and the girls and home. I don't like to think of Thanksgiving and Christmas—yet I do, and I hope you're planning some things as though I were there to share them. I will be there in my heart and mind.

Your devoted,
Colie

Colie to Ann

Sicily
Tuesday, November 16, 1943

My dearest—

So much happens in this swift-moving world that one day's vivid experience is tomorrow's dim recollection. All I can be sure of is that you have been with me in all of it, shared it as much as though you had tasted the C-rations and seen the rare blue Mediterranean with me for the first time, seen the moonlit, mountainside olive grove, breathed the keen morning air at sea.

While traveling by train through North Africa, we stopped one afternoon at a little North African town. Frank Brennan speaks French and is very proud of his success in conducting us on local tours. So we told him to go ahead and tour us.

We set out and soon an Arab in Western dress had us in tow. He seemed to be leading us to a seedy part of town, but Brennan would not hear protests, always assuming the position that any guide, as anything else he selects, is perfect. We wound up in an off-street Arab restaurant. One Arab was fat and mustached and dressed in the very important uniform of a railroad station master or some such, and he was having an animated conversation with another well dressed, European-looking, Arab. The place was very clean, though unprepossessing. The proprietor looked like a chili parlor operator. Frank's French disarmed them, so we were on friendly relations with the guests. The proprietor offered beefsteak or lamb chops. All ordered lamb chops except Craig, who said he would try a steak; but he wasted time because soon the proprietor said he had no steak, anyway. Craig said he would take an omelet and we all decided that was a good idea—we would have one, too, in addition to the chops. The omelet was good, especially if you like your eggs in a quart of olive oil; the lamb chops are funnier now than they were then. There was the least string of meat on them, a greasy string. The proprietor also brought in a spit of beef sausages to offer and they looked mighty good, but tasted like old goat. Just as we reached the peak of this rare repast, the radio came on with the news in English, an amazing development.

Most of us have learned to travel in the Dick Loeb school of tourism—that is, never eat an ordinary meal, or see a commonplace view or meet an ordinary person (in the telling). When we got back to the train we told of our sumptuous repast of omelet, wine, lamb chops, news in English, sausage, grapes, and wine—all for $1.00 each. The only difference between us and Loeb was, we laughed some about it. Dick is not with us now and I really miss him because of his enthusiasm; he can always explain everything that has happened or is about to happen and never is stumped when one of his many positive statements turns out to be wrong—as when he told us how we'd see the snow-capped mountains above Casablanca, which of course no one ever saw.

I have just had word from Washburne to meet him for supper tomorrow night. I'm delighted because old Wash is like a shot of scotch. Paths cross and recross endlessly—I have made some fine friends here and begin to realize how devoted I am to many of Charlottesville days—you hate to be parted from old pals and are delighted to see them again.

Kiss the girls for me. They are so precious and I see their faces time and again as little girls smile.

Colie

Ann to Colie

Nashville
Friday, November 19, 1943

Darling—

Every night when Carolyn says her prayers she sends you all sorts of messages—I think she feels that God will deliver them to you which is her way of letting you hear from her—for instance, give Daddy my love, tell him about Blackout.

Carolyn and Blackout.

Marie, Mort, and Sammy came over for dinner—we put all the points out and had an enormous platter of Swiss steak—at the last minute we found we had no parsley—so Archie did the decorating and you never saw anything so tempting—also had potatoes, beans, grapefruit salad, and apple pie. The only people in the house who get butter anymore are the children—so Archie fixes the margarine up like a flower—it does make it taste better.

We had a pleasant evening. The girls always enjoy Mort enormously—all the men in the family put themselves out more for the children now that you are away and it really means a lot to them.

Mother had a long cable from Briggs today—the first news in three months—he is worrying about being caught in the draft. She is all upset about it—and I have been trying to find some way to help her out with the situation. If my Junior League work these last two years has taught me nothing else, it has taught me to collect myself when a problem presents itself—though there are many times when I would give anything not to have to solve any kind of problem.

All my love,
Ann

Colie to Ann

Sicily
Friday, November 19, 1943
—For Christmas 1943

My dearest—

Christmas is more than a month away, yet it seems near at hand. I have thought of it a good deal recently because I have been thinking constantly of you and the girls, of home and all the family, and it is just one mental tuning band from there to the day that stands first of all for love and loved ones. I am alone in the apartment, it is quiet except for the occasional sound of voices on the steep, high stairway, or the slush of auto wheels in the street below. It is a welcome quiet, not a lonely one, for I came home tonight with you in my heart.

Later

Les Dawson came in and we talked about New York. Les is with Carter, Ledyard, and Milburn, an intelligent, likable fellow from my class. Then there's a knock at the door and a voice saying, "Permesso" and immediately in walk three Sicilian gentlemen. One has a note from the billeting officer saying, "Let this man look for some things in his apartment. Keep an eye on him while he's there." We hardly need the warning. He pleads that he wants to get his apartment back because his wife is going to have a baby in January, and says he has located a house of "a good friend" of his with six bedrooms and four baths and we can get it and let him return here. I say to Les in my fine Italian that I do not think our visitor is really a very close friend of the man whose house he is recommending. All three visitors laugh at this and agree the man has moved away and really isn't such a good pal.

Alden Smith.

This morning I was delighted when Alden popped in at the office. He had lunch with me and we had a good visit.

I don't know why this is a part of a Christmas letter, unless to let you know that I'll be with friends, thinking of you and home. Nothing can replace being there, but the next best thing will be thinking of you and the girls and all the family. I want you to be able to think of my Christmas here as I will be thinking of yours there, then neither of us can be as lonely as we would be without those thoughts.

Most important is that I'll have friends at hand, good friends. They will be thinking of their loved ones too, and I'm sure we'll tell one another what our families are doing. There will be a tree at the club and a bowl of merry punch. No doubt we'll sing and have turkey and fine warm friendship at every hand.

I still have my brandy and whiskey. I'm going to mix the best eggnog possible under the circumstances and have some fellows in here for a little while. I'll have your packages to open and that will be the day's high point.

Next to that, the thing I look forward to most will be taking some candy and oranges and a box of cookies and a toy to the laundry woman's children. I think it will thrill me to be able to play Santa Claus to them.

It will be a good day for me because of such things—and because I'll be thinking of you and home. I know the children will be excited over their presents, making the noises, and knowing the joys of home—the home that you and I love so much, God bless it.

We have had some happy Christmas days together, haven't we? I can remember the early ones in New York or on visits to Nashville. They were happy ones, but the best began back home in Nashville with our children. First there was Jackson Boulevard and even more in my mind, the three on Iroquois—the tree in the corner, children and toys everywhere, the door open as people came and went, then bundling everybody up to go to Grandpa's—the bustle and excitement there; Robert Mackey dropping jelly into sweet, red apples and taking an occasional look at the turkey; Mort standing before the turkey, knife glistening for the first stroke; little faces all eager and merry; joy and love and life.

I've had so much of it, I've relished it so fully. That's why I'm here, why I must be here if anyone is. I can come away from it because I carry it in my heart.

All of it is wonderful because it has all been part of you and me. In every thought of it you are radiant. I feel that I must not say so much for fear the stirring of poignant memories will overcome me with loneliness, with an anguished realization that you will not be in my arms, at my side, and everywhere before my eyes this day.

But I must say these things. I must because you are alive in my heart—you will be there forever.

When you decorate the tree or fill the stockings, when you put those magic touches to the Christmas wreath, when you watch the children, don't think I'm not there. When you read this letter, I'll be reading it over your shoulder, whispering in your ear, "I love you."

Colie

Ann to Colie

Nashville
Wednesday, November 24, 1943

Darling—

Sam brought us a live turkey Monday afternoon. Archie put him in the pigeon house, because we don't want to eat him until next week—Mr. O'Brien has a flock of them next door that he is raising—so I went out to ask him what to feed this one of ours. It seems that corn is the best, but there is none to be bought. To make a long story short, Mr. O. has taken our turkey under his wing and is feeding him with his corn—he is the most neighborly person imaginable. I can see him out the window now—his flock love to nibble in our yard—which they do everyday—so he is out looking after them. He was talking to me yesterday—said we ought to have the entire orchard plowed up to kill the insects in the ground. I was wondering if it might not be dangerous to the roots of the fruit trees. He said no—said there will always be some of us who can see that it is done right. A dandy kind of neighbor to have.

All my love, darling—
Ann

Ann to Colie

Nashville
Wednesday, November 24, 1943

Darling—

I've suddenly realized that if you were going to have a Christmas letter from me—I had better write it now.

I have thought so much about our Christmas days together—I remember the first one on 72nd Street when you slipped in the kitchen and made me an eggnog. We've traveled a busy road since then—remember last year—the first Christmas in our grand new house. I find it hard to realize life was ever so placid, so full. Now the days are full of feverish activity—and so much of it flat because our husbands are away. I try to remind myself that we have so many blessings—and we have. God has been good to America—I'm far from complaining—but I want you to know, too, how empty the days are without you.

When you read this the children will be busy around the tree, and I hope Mort will be sampling some of our eggnog! I am determined to carry on the tradition and have a bowl of nog. I don't know where we will be for Christmas dinner—probably Grandpa's—Rob and Jane are having their party again that night.

I shall have you in my heart every minute of the day—It's hard for me to realize that we won't be together—And I'm hoping you and Alden will manage some sort of celebration—I'm proud of you and I love you—"God bless you and keep you—may his face shine upon you and be gracious unto you."

Devotedly,
Ann

Colie to Sam K. Harwell Sr.

Sicily
Thursday, November 25, 1943

Dear Father—

One month from tonight will be Christmas. In a way that seems far off, but in another way it seems very close at hand. I have thought a great deal recently of Christmas because all the members of the family have been in my mind and when I think of those I love most I think of the gatherings we have had, the happy times, at Christmas. I am asking Sam to deliver this letter to you. It will have to substitute this year for the neckties. I looked at some here but they were not worthy of your taste. So I hope you'll forgive the absence of a present this year.

It is hard to realize that I have been away from home six months. I think I could pull up a chair before your fire tonight and feel that I had just been out in the cold a while. This is not because I haven't missed your fireside and each one who shares its warmth, missed you continually, but because the warmth seems to be always with me. This is, I believe, one of the longest periods I have ever been away from home. But home stays in my heart. I know every member of our family, of your family, shares with me in gratitude for the bright memories of home that stay with us always, no matter how long or how distant our travel.

I have had experiences in recent weeks I couldn't have dreamed of a year ago. I have made many friends and seen many places I never expected to know better than in headlines. It is vastly interesting and

I am thankful for the good luck that has brought me this close to doing a part of the job, however small—I know how many would like to be this fortunate.

As you know, I came this way because I felt I had to if there was a place I could do a job. Never for a moment have I doubted that was the right thing for me to do. For confidence in that decision, I know and appreciate how much I have relied on the support that is essential—from you, from Ann, from Sam and Rob, from Sister, from my little girls, from all the family—and, from the start, that support has never failed.

Rob wrote me a letter recently in which he recalled the times, at various stages of the past, when I played soldier. I remember those with fondness and gratitude—Peabody and Ridgetop and Muskegong, Michigan, and I think those play days did a lot to condition me for this experience. Sleeping on canvas in the ship's hold or in the baggage rack of the train, being thrown in suddenly with a bunch of youngsters in a position of command at camp, finding myself now in uniform in this distant land, all has come rather easily. But the more important conditioning, I believe, was in the teachings of our home. If I have been able to take such slight hardships and face such small challenges as have come my way, it was due to that—and to all the good things that have been my fortune.

In writing this Christmas message to you, I feel in a way that I am writing it to every member of the family. When I think of all the good things for which I can thank you, I also think of each one there and how much I owe to them. Most of all I think of how remarkable it is that the memory of your red chair and fireside includes so many people and that the picture is not complete without them all.

My greatest comfort is in knowing that Ann and our little girls are part of that picture—that they are in your heart and the hearts of all who are there. And that all of you are in their hearts. The same spirit is there for them that we have known since we were little.

I remember many things about Christmas in our home on West End. I can almost count the pieces of candy I poured out of my

The Harwell boys and their mother, circa 1912. Left to right: Sam Jr., Coleman, Leila McClure Harwell, Goodrum (standing), and Rob.

stocking; the time when I got the coaster wagon and we pulled the turkey in on it; how the orange was always in the tip of the stocking and a peppermint stick cane at the top, except once when there was something else and it turned out to be a ring in a box—I woke Mother to show it to her; how we serenaded Hortense with our horns and drums and she got mad and threatened to quit and I think you had to double her Christmas gift. I don't know how you and Mother stood it for it seems to me it went on and grew noisier for years. I remember a good deal about those Christmases, but mostly I remember the spirit of our home. I think I understand that spirit better now than ever.

I remember that Mother was very beautiful and such an easy person to be with. She was good company and always interested in everything and everybody. She never neglected one of us for another and yet she was concerned with all that touched any of us; she gave her undivided attention to any little problem of mine just as though it were something very important. I remember we burned the commons once, and Sam and Rob were in the thick of it, so I was, too. I must have been small and not known how dangerous it was, for she finally got me in and scolded me severely and then cried about it. When she went to the Peabody PTA, that was the one thing on her mind; she entertained Miss Lillian Taylor and our third grade of Tarbox [School] as though we were the most important group anywhere, and for that reason we were. When I went to Vanderbilt to make an oration in a contest, she went with me. I made a terrible speech but she said I was good and that was enough for me.

I remember you sitting by the fire in your big chair and wanting your slippers. I knew then as I know now that was the one place in the world you wanted to be. Now I feel just that way about my wife and children and home. That's the way Sister feels about her home and family, and Sam and Rob about theirs.

There are many glorious memories of our home that come back most clearly at this time of year. The wonderful times when we had the Knoxes with us, the memories of the first Christmas when another generation came along to add to our happiness and to share it—first Mortie, then Sammy and Evalina and Leila, then Buddy and Robin lying side by side as little fellows, then Ann McClure and Carolyn and Jonathan, and now there's a bright new face this year. I think often of Miss Evie's wonderful friendship and the happy times with her, how glad she was to have us visit each time, how much she did for our happiness.

Not separate in our hearts, but there as though they'd always been, are those who've stepped into the scene and become a part of it, Mort and Josephine, Jane and Ann. Not them alone, but those they love as well. To me as to Ann, it has meant much that her mother and Briggs have come to be a part of the scene, to share the love we've known there.

So, when Christmas is near, I sit in a large, barren room in Sicily, while my English roommate snores away and the still night is broken outside by the rumbling of an army truck—and think of you in your red chair and Robert Mackey bringing in another stick for the fire. That's why I think of all those who will be with you and those whose hearts will be there.

Homesick? Well, I wouldn't deny it, but my heart is so full of thankfulness for happy memories and the love I've shared, there isn't much room left for loneliness. As you think of me this Christmas day, know that I'm fortunate to be with good friends. We'll have packages from home to open, turkey dinner with all the trimmings, and I'm certain there'll be a flowing bowl. With these and the thoughts of home, I'll have a far from empty day.

I don't know if you'll have the full gathering at your house. But whether you do or not, I hope you'll give my love and Christmas greetings to all the family. I wish that Mortie and Nancy, Sammy and Briggs and I could be there. My greatest wish is for the day when we will all be together with you again.

I'd like to drop in on Christmas morning; to see Mackey take one final survey of the turkey; to see Mort at his alert before the first smooth stroke; to hear the babble in the hallway and see the eager little faces awaiting the dreamed of bounty.

I am thankful for having known such happiness, for having it in my heart today. Bless you all, from you to baby Colie and back again. And, with all my heart,

Merry Christmas!

Devotedly,
Colie

Colie to Ann

Sicily
Tuesday, November 30, 1943

My dearest—

Yesterday I finally got off the box I've been wanting to mail a long while. It will take about two months to reach you, but while I have it in mind, I'd better write you a list of what's in it. Most of the things are for the children.

There's a little Sicilian tea set for you, a commonplace sort of thing but apparently the linen is all right and I think it would do for very informal use, a children's party or the like. There are four handkerchiefs, for your mother, for Sister, Josephine, and Jane. Also for you are three Sicilian carts. They range from tiny to toy size and I thought you might want to use them in the secretary, but it may be you think they'll be better for the children's rooms. Every cart in Sicily (and they are used in both city and on the farm) is painted with a historic scene on a bright yellow background.

For all the children there are tiny children's books in Italian. They have cute drawings in them and I thought even Evalina and Leila would like to have them as souvenirs. Look through them and select them for the various ones, Evalina, Leila, Buddy, Robin, Jonathan, Clurie, and Carolyn. You might let Clurie and Carolyn decide how to distribute them. Then, for the girls there are two dolls and two dresses for them (the girls, not the dolls). They are simple little Sicilian smock effects for summer, I suppose. Then there is what I hope is a pretty dress for baby Colie. Hope my next shipment will be better; hope this reaches there before too long.

With all my love,
Colie

Colie to Ann

Sicily
Tuesday, November 30, 1943

My dearest—

You can imagine how happy I've been to have Harry Cain in the bunk beside mine. His rich, rasping brogue has been the source of much delight to me again and his experiences have delighted me thoroughly. They have been as many and as colorful as you, knowing Harry, would expect. Last night he and Sansome and I went to a movie and afterwards sat with several others drinking a mixture of cognac and Marsala wine and munching some cakes Fred had brought, and talking about all these things we are thinking and doing. It was a bull session of the best order, with current topics first on the list, but interspersed with talk of the old days just enough to give it that flavor of friendship that makes life worthwhile.

Here's worlds of love to you and the girls.

With all my heart,
Colie

On December 1, Colie left Sicily, on his way to Italy.

Italy—Arrival

On December 1, Coleman Harwell arrived in Naples, where he became a Public Relations Officer with AMG.

Colie to Ann

Italy
Wednesday, December 1, 1943

My dearest—

How addresses do change! So swiftly sometimes I have to remind myself where I am. I light a cigarette, get well into an overseas copy of *Life*—and there is Italy. More beautiful than anything I've seen. And I'm glad to be here to do a job—one that interests me a great deal and for which I hope and believe I am well equipped.

Colie

Ann to Colie

Nashville
Friday, December 3, 1943

Darling—

Carolyn is now downstairs riding around on the tricycle and talking every minute. She is so sociable. Mother says Carolyn is the

Martha of the Bible—which I believe indicates the homebody, the housekeeper. She is making up the doll bed and trying to sing "Sur le Pont d'Avignon."

Mother has given us our living room curtains for Christmas and Mr. Rodgers hung them yesterday. They have a blue background with large roses and bow knots on them. Really lovely. It is hard for me to get interested in the furnishings with you gone—but Mother is getting behind me—and insists on doing a few things to make up for room and board.

Last night Clurie had a loose tooth—but we couldn't get it out. So this morning when she woke up the tooth was gone, which we all thought was pretty funny. She had evidently swallowed it. She says it was like swallowing a dime—because of course now the tooth fairy won't leave any money.

I have finished the Gray Lady course and we are waiting for our uniforms to come so we can be veiled—then we go on duty. I can only manage one afternoon a week, but hope to do more when I finish my Junior League work. I am glad the course is over—three afternoons a week was rather onerous, as you can imagine.

It is dreadful having you away—but more and more I look with pride on it and realize that you couldn't have done otherwise—nor would I really want you to. It would have been wonderful to have you doing your bit somewhere in this country—but at the same time I know that would not have satisfied you and I understand that too. So although I might as well admit that the sledding is pretty rough without you, I want you to remember that I am perfectly sure you are doing the only thing that a person of your high standards could do. All I ask is that your work satisfy you. Then when this maelstrom is over, we will feel that we have well earned our happiness together. And what a glorious time that will be—I don't dare let my mind dwell on it too much; I might lose strength for the long road that must be traveled first.

Devotedly,
Ann

Archie Buchanan to Colie

Nashville
Friday, December 3, 1943

Dear Mr. Capt. Harwell—

I meet the mailman every day to see if Mrs. Harwell gets a letter from you and find out how you are. I sure miss you for I felt that you were my best friend and will be glad when it is over and you come back home again that will be a happy meeting. Lots of good luck and everything.

Merry Christmas,
Archie Buchanan

Ann to Colie

Nashville
Sunday, December 5, 1943

Darling—

My weekend has been quiet with the exception of a game of bridge last night. Enid, Dibbie, and I had dinner at the club—then Florence Fletcher joined us for a game here.

The Sam Harwells came over and had dinner with us today—all five of them. We had one of Grandpa's beef roasts which we had kept frozen in the refrigerator for a week, and it was wonderful. Their cook has been sick all week—so I think they doubly appreciated the invitation. Sam has been marvelous about bringing me things—such as oranges. I never know when I get home what he will have come by and brought.

You have seemed so close lately. You've only been gone a little over three months, but I feel that it has been half my life. Did I tell you that Goode Davis had been here on leave after being away over a year? He is supposed to have told Martha that he thought she would look middle-aged but she didn't. So I'm wondering what all you other husbands expect to find us like when you get home. I don't feel old in body—only in responsibility.

Ann

Colie to Ann

Italy
Sunday, December 5, 1943

My dearest—

I've just moved to new living quarters. When Allen Austin and Ken Curran asked me to move in with them I was quite pleased. You remember Curran, I believe—a very sober and studious Princeton professor of economics; Austin is a Cleveland engineer. I never knew them well at Charlottesville, but traveling the same road so long brings you closer to people.

The couple living here had an old cook named Assunta who stays on with us and we have the place fully furnished. There is a nice small living room, a pleasant dining room, two bedrooms, kitchen, bath and maid's room, and a parlor which I have just finished making over into my bedroom. It is full of the startling colors, tapestry, pictures, and bric-a-brac that middle-class Italians love. The dining room has a dark oak banquet table that will seat ten, a heavy sideboard and buffet to match, heavy iron chandelier, a maroon finished wall that seems to be brocade, a very pretty cream and white decorated ceiling, and stone floor of a fancy design. The radio is in here and we use it mainly as our living room. My bedroom has an upright piano, a china cupboard crammed with curios and is finished in a bilious orange tint. We moved in a big cupboard, moved out a hard sofa and two of the chairs and brought in a comfortable chair from the living room. Also one of the never-to-be-overlooked night tables (for ye olde potte) and a bed I secured through one of our offices. We pay $40 a month rent and pay Assunta $6 a month. That, of course, is much more in terms of 600 lire and she has good quarters and is well fed. Allen bought a heater today for $14, but it is comfortable tonight without it. Added attractions: a cuckoo clock in the dining room that works four times every hour and a cat with whom Assunta keeps up a constant conversation.

Wish this "trip" were different—that you were here to share this glorious scene. It takes your breath away when, for an instant, the constant scenes of warfare fade out and you see only the wonders of God's and man's creations. Love to all of you.

Colie

Colie to Ann

Italy

Monday, December 6, 1943

My dearest—

I had started writing you when the sound of "Fibber McGee and Molly" and "The Great Gildersleeve" interrupted and I had to come into the dining room to hear them. They were kidding Gildersleeve about proposing and I enjoyed the delightful feeling of real life that they brought back—now Kay Kyser is on. How many times we've enjoyed them together; they've brought home to me as I'm sure they have to millions of others. A special station broadcasts the best American programs as well as British and BBC news. (We can get German and other distant stations too.) Tonight at dinner we heard the BBC broadcast the Roosevelt-Churchill-Stalin statement. The meeting was the most dramatic and meaningful of our age and I'm sure it has thrilled you as it did me.

I enjoy my work more each day. If I do not learn from it, I never will from anything. At the same time, I hope I'm lucky enough to make some small contribution to the big job we have. I'm enjoying my surroundings tremendously. The dinner we had tonight buoyed my morale 100%. Delicious ham and French fried potatoes, spinach, excellent bread, jam and marmalade, cocoa, and some of those wonderful canned peaches your rationing made possible. Assunta is an excellent cook and cheery as a kettle. Also she did beautiful laundry for Allen. Allen and Ken are fine apartment mates, businesslike and considerate and good company, too.

All my love,

Colie

Colie to Ann

Italy
Tuesday, December 7, 1943

My dearest—

I remember as clearly as yesterday what happened two years ago today—the bright morning, the excitement when I gave you the birthday "note," you and the girls so pleased when the final message led you to the garage and the shiny new blue car. Then the afternoon, sitting down to lunch, the phone call, "the Japs have blasted our navy out of Pearl Harbor"—the rush to the office, an extra at 4:30, then wirephotos and more extras, more editions. Most of all I remember you knew as certainly as anyone could what it meant to you and me; at last it was true and I would go if there was any place I could serve. You knew that before I did. You wouldn't have wanted me to do anything else. Your birthday—how thankful I am for it. I wish I could bring out champagne to drink to you and with you. But, far more important, I can thank God for you. My life gained new meaning on this day of yours, so I celebrate it thankfully and save the kisses, the many kisses, until some happy day in the future.

Devotedly,
Colie

Rob Harwell wrote Colie on December 10 that, during a recent visit to New York, he and Jane had tended to Colie's request to purchase furs for Ann for Christmas. "The responsibility finally was left with Jane," he noted. "Ann had expressed privately that she did not want a fur coat, but that she did want a fur scarf. The scarf which Jane selected for her is three Hudson Bay sables. They are very unusual and very fine, something that could last Ann the rest of her life and something that she will always be proud of."

Ann to Colie

Friday, December 10, 1943

Darling—

The world of unreality you are living in must at times seem very strange. It could hardly be otherwise. I think then of you who have left your own world to carry on with this new existence. You should feel very proud of what you are doing. You say you couldn't do otherwise, and I understand that too. But in my heart I know it isn't easy—I want you to know that I realize what it means—and I want you to know that I am standing behind you in all of it—You should never feel lonely or discouraged because I am always with you— knowing you can do whatever the job may be—loving you every minute of the day and night, holding alive in my heart all the things that mean so much because they are yours and mine.

Devotedly,

Ann

Colie wrote in his diary in early December that "PROing gives you a new appreciation of the press. A half-hour story in the news room is a two-day job here." By December 13, he had "conducted [his] first press conference for Col. Hume, on announcement of abolition of syndicates. Seemed to go well and correspondents' attitude indicated sympathetic reaction. Maj. Boettiger later expressed satisfaction with my approach to the job as a whole which was a most welcome encouragement."

Ann to Colie

Nashville

Tuesday, December 14, 1943

Darling—

I've had Briggs's problem very much on my mind—it looks as though he is going to have to return for induction. I have been in the middle—and have taken the responsibility rather hard—I feel as though I had been through an illness. It seems that I am always carrying somebody's load for them—I don't feel that my shoulders are that strong or my judgment that good.

Sammy is now at a field near where Mortie is—so the Howells are going down for Christmas. We will miss them here—as I told Mort, the eggnog is never as good when he isn't here to talk about it and taste each sip with relish. Robert Mackey and Grandpa are going ahead with plans for the family dinner there—I'm glad because it means so much to the children.

You've never seen anything like the money being spent here for Christmas—the stores are so crowded you can scarcely get through the aisles—and people seem to be buying everything—no matter what the cost or value received.

Mother and I went to the Wilsons for supper Sunday night—we left about 11:00—I had trouble getting the car started—but thought it was just cold—so drifted on down the drive into the middle of Chickering Road—only to discover I was completely out of gas. It was impossible to get gas that time of night—and I was afraid to leave the car there for fear someone would steal the tires—so I had an inspiration and called the Belle Meade police—They came immediately and pushed me all the way home—quite a stunt.

Devotedly,
Ann

Ann to Colie

Nashville
Saturday, December 18, 1943

Darling—

Last night Warren had a surprise birthday party for Martine—he and the cook planned everything even to hot canapes with the drinks—the drinks incidentally were some sort of fancy brew mixed up twenty-four hours in advance and packed a terrific wallop—which I didn't realize until this morning. Present were Teeny, Ann Light, Lucy, Ed Keebles, Rob Harwells, and Bitsy Wilsons—We all did a lot of talking—and had a good time. Rob was in his Christmas day mood and insisted not only on telling us the entire story of

Oklahoma but playing all the records besides. Jane says he is trying to carry on for you by being the life of the party.

Devotedly,
Ann

Colie to Ann

Italy
Saturday, December 18, 1943

My dearest—

This is a very domestic, tranquil scene tonight. Allen is working on a report; Ken is writing a note in Italian to our landlord. The note is in answer to one Allen received today saying that there were two young orphan *signorinas* whose Christmas could be brightened by a charitable deed from *il buon capitano*. Assunta advised us that the young *signorinas* were about 25 or 30 years of age, which confused our plans to get up a box of candy and buy some little clothes for them. The landlord, however, is a nice old gent, so we feel sure his intentions are honest and we are asking him just how badly off the sisters are and what we can do for them.

John Clarke and Joe Hickingbotham have an apartment on a hill above us and we plan to have them down and to visit them, too. John swears he's going to have a turkey if he has to shoot it himself. I hope he has better luck than he has had trying to get a car. You know he wouldn't go to the bathroom in Charlottesville without his Cadillac and it's been killing him over here not to have any transportation. I think he has walked more in the last week than he's walked in the previous thirty years. He wants to buy one and has the cash ready to drop in a second, but cars can't be found. Distances are fairly great so it is a serious matter for us, and lots of others, too. But there are some funny angles.

Devotedly,
Colie

VETERAN'S ADMINISTRATION HOSPITAL, THAYER MEMORIAL, NASHVILLE, TENN.

Thayer Hospital, where Ann Harwell served as a Gray Lady.

Ann to Colie

Nashville
Monday, December 20, 1943

Darling—

Clurie and I went in town this morning at 9:00 to get our hair washed so we would be ready for the holiday—then I rushed home to change into my Gray Lady uniform so I could spend the rest of the day at Thayer—putting Christmas decorations all through the hospital—Jo Harwell is a Gray Lady too—and we worked as a team today fixing up three wards—the patients who were able helped us and we thought they looked pretty good when we finished—but were we tired. After dinner tonight I found I was supposed to go to town tomorrow to help wrap candy for the party the Colonial Dames have for the boys on Christmas Eve—and I'm having fourteen people in for dinner tomorrow—so I'm writing this in between making the salad and the mayonnaise. I wanted to be busy so there wouldn't be much time to think and I certainly am.

Devotedly,
Ann

Colie to Ann

Italy
Wednesday, December 22, 1943

My dearest—

Tonight we are supposed to have our first Italian lesson with a young *professoressa* discovered by Assunta. Ken made the initial call last night and reports she is a very nice young girl, about 19, and thoroughly safe since Mama hangs around all the time. She speaks English well, has read much English literature, and is very pleased at the prospect of teaching us. We are to pay her for lessons three nights a week, but the price was not settled on. The idea seems to be not to discuss the money part and to send the remittance by Assunta. That is a favorite way the Italians have of handling things, probably because they've found Americans more inclined to overpay than underpay.

Devotedly,
Colie

Colie to Ann

Italy
Friday, December 24, 1943

My dearest—

It is now 9:45—we have heard Christmas carols broadcast from a German radio station—then we shifted to our station and heard the President's Christmas message—now we pause to hear a very fine reading of "The Night Before Christmas"—Al is writing a letter, Ken is reading, we feel very lucky in this area now to have light and a pleasant room, good company, on Christmas Eve.

I am thinking of what you are doing now, how you will spend this Christmas Eve—the girls hanging their stockings, perhaps some of the family dropping in, your mother decorating the tree (I wish I could mix a light toddy to spur on the occasion). These things are in my heart and mind, as thoughts of you are always. God bless you this night.

We had our children's party today. There were fifteen jammed around the dining room table—the cutest little things you ever saw.

There was a darling little girl, five, named Vittoria, and a brash, bright-eyed boy, Tony. Also one of the most gorgeous little girls, about three, you've ever seen, and I remarked she was much too pretty to be good. She began hitting the little girl next to her when the eating ended and we had to separate them. We had jelly on bread, hot chocolate, hard candies. They behaved beautifully under the guidance of their mothers and nurses. I believe they would correspond closely to the children Clurie and Carolyn would have to a party, and that made it even more pleasing to me. They had been well coached to say "good-a night," and "Buon Natale" and were cherubic as they bid their good nights. Our *professoressa* helped arrange the party. She stayed afterward and ate pasta with us (homemade by Assunta) and we talked Italian an hour.

After she left, we listened to the radio and Al broke out a half pint of Scotch which furnished us with two drinks each, and we talked about home and Christmas.

Assunta has a small spruce tree decorated with bright papers and three oranges, and the dining-living room is quite Christmasy.

There's a place far away where I wish I could be tonight. The moon is shining there, there are snow crystals on the windows, two little girls are hanging their stockings and soon they'll say a prayer for their Daddy far away—the sweetest wife in all the world is thinking, as I am, of Christmases that have been and that will be.

God bless you and keep you—

Merry Christmas—

Your devoted husband,
Colie

Christmas

Colie to Ann
Christmas Day, Saturday, December 25, 1943

My dearest—

No one could hope to be as lucky as I have been in all the marvelous reminders of those who are in my heart today. Most wonderful of all was the folder of snapshots. That alone would have brought joy to me. In addition to that are all the things I wanted—a treasure of books, especially the Shakespeare volume and *c/o Postmaster*. Then the grand pen-pencil set. Many other things—your fruit cake, the pudding from the office, knife, flashlights—the comic package Rob sent of false teeth, monkey, phony candy, all of which have seen service already. I received six packages yesterday, bringing my total to fourteen, an amazing number. Tell Clurie and Carolyn their presents were perfect.

With all my heart,
Colie

P.S. Tradition lives and I mixed the morning eggnog with condensed milk, powdered eggs, touch of Bourbon and rum. We had it before breakfast—everyone said it was good, including Assunta!

Ann to Colie

Nashville
Sunday, December 26, 1943

My darling—

The sables are gorgeous—and how long I have wanted some—
never really expecting the day to come when I would actually own
anything so lovely. I wore them last night proudly, defiantly—I felt
almost as though it were your arm around my shoulders—they gave
me new courage to get through a day that was almost more than I
could manage. And the orchid—with your card in your own hand-
writing—it was as though you had spoken to me across the
miles—and had wrapped me in the warmth of your love—the love
that means more to me than anything in life—it's the one thing I
cling to, the one thing that gives me courage and strength to go on
with each day.

I couldn't write you yesterday—it's hard enough today—but I
must let you know the things that are in my heart—the brave front
must crumble at times. We've always made so much of Christmas
and without you—well, you know how I felt. Your wonderful letter I
read before Christmas—I had to, and I'm glad because I couldn't
have read it yesterday and still gone on. The letter to your father was
so sweet—Sam read it aloud to us after dinner—you were so very
thoughtful—Mother was so touched by your flowers—we both
stood in the kitchen sniffling like babies—and all the others you
remembered—how wonderful of you to do it.

The children had a wonderful day—Carolyn started out the day
by saying she felt sick—so I made her lie down in the playroom
where she promptly fell asleep and stayed for an hour—then when
she came to, she was completely revived and finished up the rest of
the day in great style. Whenever I felt a low coming on I took a good
look at Carolyn in her WAC outfit—the skirt kept slipping down and
the cap would get completely turned around on her head—hair
flying in every direction—she was the cutest thing I ever saw. Clurie

Clurie, Carolyn, and Sandra McNeill, Christmas 1943.

has taken hers off only long enough to sleep. They loved having a present from you. We opened the African packages and they got out the adorable little shoes. I gave the wallets to Sam, Rob, and Grandpa—I should have liked to have kept one but you had already given me such a wonderful Christmas—and I thought it might be a comfort to Grandpa. He has had a bad cold, but has not been in bed—just sits in his red chair. We had a marvelous dinner there yesterday—the Howells are away—so Robert Mackey did it all alone.

Yesterday we managed to make a bowl of nog and have the family and the McNeills in for a little cheer. Then last night we went to Rob and Jane's—it was a good party but there were so many absent, there didn't seem to be quite the same feeling.

Devotedly,
Ann

Ann to Colie

Nashville
Tuesday, December 28, 1943

Darling—

Mr. Evans sent us a dressed turkey Christmas Eve—and I was afraid not to use it right away—Mother is in Columbia—so Dibbie came up and ate turkey with the girls and me—it was delicious—We sat knitting and listening to the radio until Bob Hope finished.

Warren has been taken into the Rotary Club and today was the luncheon for the children—He invited our girls to go with him and Sandra—there was a magician and they had a marvelous time.

I heard Clurie telling Mannie yesterday, "Daddy gave Mummy some furs and they're *stables*." Really they are so lovely—I'm hoping it won't be too long before you can see them for yourself.

Ann

Ann to Colie

Nashville
Wednesday, December 29, 1943

Darling—

The *Tennessean* office party was at the Hermitage Hotel again this year. A good many of the staff had sent cards to me—and all were very much interested in hearing about you. Just as I was getting ready to go, Mr. Evans had McDowell play "Over There" for you and had me come to the mike and make a little speech—which was nothing more than Merry Christmas—because by that time I was ready to burst into tears. He is continuously going out of his way to make me feel that I am a vital part of the organization—and I do appreciate it.

This afternoon the lights in my room and Clurie's got so dim as to be almost imperceptible and are still that way—also the ovens on the stove refused to heat and the refrigerator has gone on the blink— so I am going to have to get an electrician here first thing in the morning. I had a man put new valves on some of the radiators and you have never seen such a complete change—Carolyn and Clurie's rooms get so hot sometimes we actually have to shut off the heat—

the kitchen which has had no heat in it all year is the same way—and even the library is warm. So I am planning to have them put on all the others as well—they cost $2 each—but what a relief.

I've been meaning to tell you about Blackout—I gave him away to Mrs. Wair and her little boys who adore him and have a fenced in backyard. He was simply driving me crazy—running off every day—people would pick him up then call me at eleven o'clock at night to come and get him. The last time a man called from way over on Charlotte Pike and said he had no place to keep him. I couldn't go over there at that hour of the night alone. So the next morning early I got our neighbor Mr. O'Brien and was ready to start out when someone else called and said he was at Cohn School. So we got him and kept him locked up until I gave him away. I felt almost as though I were losing a member of the family.

Mother is back from Columbia today—rather tired and worrying a good deal about Briggs. It was like working with a shadow—with expensive cables flying back and forth. Some day I'm going to work with an organization where I can talk to my heart's content and not always have to be so discreet—now I'm in the middle of the Gray Ladies where you have a very strict code of ethics. What I could tell about everything if I ever let myself go—I don't mean in regard to the Gray Ladies—but all sorts of other things—and now I have to even worry about what I write you because of the censor. And Mother—who thinks she is discreet—just simply doesn't know the meaning of the word—so I am a badly inhibited female.

All my love,
Ann

Colie to Ann

Italy
Wednesday, December 29, 1943

My dearest—

More about Christmas. After I wrote you, I walked home. A brisk, beautiful walk it was—marred by terrible scars of war, shattered homes and shattered hopes for a time, but signs of restoration, friendly smiles on the faces of soldiers and civilians, many Good Mornings and Buon Natales and Merry Christmases.

Enroute I stopped at the British-American Church for an appealing Christmas program. A splendid choir of Britishers sang "God Rest You Merry Gentlemen"—the congregation joined in "Holy Night" and other carols. Then home, and to open three packages I had not had a chance to open the day before. The prize was the photo album from the office, its jewels being you and Clurie and Carolyn in that luscious photo—I cannot tell you how much it has meant to me.

Devotedly,
Colie

Colie to Ann

Italy
Wednesday, December 29, 1943

My dearest—

I'm afraid my hopes of finding Assunta to be a good cook are cooked. The poor thing has to devote her mental capacity to giving us something hot on the one electric eye and the charcoal burner that smokes up the kitchen so badly she can hardly stay in it. She did come through with a fair salad of mixed vegetables and potatoes, with a weird concoction of powdered-egg mayonnaise. Generally, though, we have a good soup or pasta dish first. Tonight she made a rice dish (from our ration rice) that was very good, as a substitute for soup. Then we have a big dish of G-I meat (spam, viennas) or sometimes a piece of fresh beef, and a mixture of fried vegetables, potatoes, *finochio*, and carrots. Then a bit of fresh salad. Accompanied by hot chocolate and bread and jam or marmalade. Dessert is sometimes canned fruit, sometimes just the fruit and nuts with which we always end. There is a hotel near us where we go occasionally to have a G-I dinner. Of course, there are no restaurants open at night and this hotel, like most others, is operated by the army.

Guess what? John Clarke has a car! The other night he came by to bring me home and we laughed all the way. It is a Fiat and Clarke looks like an undertaker driving it. It shimmies all over the road and has every sort of contrivance, but Clarke is so happy to be off his feet I think he would have settled for a jackass. The three of us went to dinner up there the other night. He is living in the town apartment of a duke, and he has had the rare good luck of getting a very good cook, Amelia.

Clarke and I had a wonderful laugh when he showed us his private cache of belongings—more shirts and underwear and socks and towels than you ever saw outside a store, and eighty bars of soap. Funny thing about it is, however, that you never are willing to quit buying, for you never know when you'll come up against a time when you can't get any more.

I am so very proud of you and all you are doing. I hope you like the Gray Lady course, for it is something you will do to perfection. I am glad it gives you a feeling of a part in the war more directly, but I appreciate more than anyone how very much you are doing, in so many different and important ways already. Our home is such an important part of that, what you mean to so many people, your tremendous responsibility at the Junior League Home. You must have an idea of how much heart you give to me, how much it means to me in this far, strange place, to have you and your love, your strength and courage behind me—most of all, your love. I have realized more and more how rare it is to share such love and courage and beauty.

I will write Walton Garrett about your having more money, but there is no reason for you not to have whatever you need at any time. If any considerable amounts are necessary and you feel hesitant about them, feel free to discuss them with Father, Sam, or Rob. I know sometimes they seem rushed, but faced directly, any of them can give you the best of advice and they are all fully aware of my finances. I think it would be well to try to get Sam to come sometime to discuss plowing up the orchard. He is the best adviser on such matters I know of. You are wise to plan a small garden. I think you should get some grass seed out on the yard and on the garden area you plan to seed with grass soon. I am very little help from such a distance, but I do appreciate your writing me these details. You know whatever you do has my second.

Devotedly,
Colie

CHAPTER TWELVE

A New Year

Ann to Colie

Nashville
Saturday, January 1, 1944

Darling—

It is almost impossible to realize that we have been in this war over two years. Lip Davis was saying that it didn't seem possible that you could have left over seven months ago—it seems much longer to me. If someone had seen this in the cards for me, I would have said that I couldn't stand up under it. But as I laughingly said to Sam the other day when we were talking about so many people having flu—I said the Lord had been looking after me—and Sam replied, "If you just lean on Him, He will."

Bobby and Ed had a bunch of us up to their house last night—we had dinner and ushered in the new year. It was a quiet party rather than the usual frenzy. My Christmas orchid was still in perfect condition so I looked elegant whether I felt it or not. Einer was amazed at the orchid—thought you had sent me another one. I am still like a child with a new toy with my sables—I never expect to find them routine. My favorite story is about my lame shoulder. Archie wasn't

95

here for three days at Christmas time and the job of stoking the furnace went to me. Monday night when I went out to dinner I had an extremely painful shoulder, could scarcely turn my head. I said I didn't know if it was from putting coal in the stoker or from squaring off my shoulders to wear the sables. I think the general feeling was that it was due to the sables. Jane said I sat perfectly rigid most of Christmas night—wearing my hat and also the orchid and with the sables wound firmly around my neck.

I love you,
Ann

Ann to Colie

Nashville
Tuesday, January 4, 1944

Darling—

Everyone is well—Grandpa's cold seems about gone and I think he will be out tomorrow—Mackey has been sick since Christmas and that has thrown the house into a turmoil. They got Miss Wall, an R.N., to come out and nurse Grandpa but really just to be there so he wouldn't be alone—however, I understood from the Howells last night that she was not going to stay—just between you and me it is going to be hard to get someone who can be companionable and of service at the same time, because Grandpa demands so much—as Sam says he turns everybody into a servant. However, when Mackey gets back I'm sure everything will take on a brighter hue. Grandpa doesn't seem disturbed by any of it, so that helps.

Remember always how much I love you.

Ann

Colie to Ann

Italy
Wednesday, January 5, 1944

My dearest—

The monotony of our recent meals was broken tonight as Al came back from the QM [Quarter Master] with a cut of fresh meat of about ten pounds—round steak, I suppose it was. Assunta cooked a part of it which we had after a soup made of bouillon cubes Al had received for Christmas, peas and beets, then the crown jewel of peaches. I topped all that with a round of Italian walnuts under the lash of Assunta's vigorous tableside cracking, then a huge piece of your Mitchell's chocolate.

Every time we have canned fruit I know how much you and the children would enjoy it and realize we're having it because you are not. That goes for so many things, especially the steak we had tonight. I think I'm right in saying that soldiers everywhere eat well and sufficiently. I think the people at home ought to know they're making it possible.

Last night Main Albright came to dinner and was delighted to find it was our evening of instruction from the *professoressa*. It always startles me to realize that a twenty-year-old girl can handle us as she does. She talks to us like the schoolboys we are, yet shows the respect you'd expect a well-bred young lady to show her "elders," and has that way you find often in Southern girls of being completely at ease, yet a perfect lady.

When we got home last night, Assunta gave us a package which she said *La Donna* (Grandmother) of the *professoressa* had brought. In it were three little china, dimestore shoes. They were gifts of Befana, which the Italians celebrate as their gift day—the day on which the wise men brought gifts to Christ. Christmas Day is almost entirely a religious occasion with them, the real celebration is Befana and on that day the children receive shoes (instead of stockings) with good things in them. The bad children receive coal and potatoes. Each of us had a piece of coal and a piece of potato, as well as trinket toys of fish, dogs, etc. In response, we fixed a Christmas sock for her with a bar of chocolate, packages of hard candies and, I'm sure most welcome of all, very practical gifts of soap bars, a box of powder, a carton of safety matches, and a couple of packages of cigarettes.

My Christmas jackpot has been paying big dividends. Most enjoyable has been my reacquaintance with Shakespeare. Reading *King Lear* the last day or so, I've even read several passages out loud and Al and Ken enjoyed it as much as I did. Two lines struck home tonight: "The art of our necessities is strange, That can make vile things precious." He was considering sleeping on a straw pile after coming in from the rain.

With all my heart,
Colie

Ann to Colie

Nashville
Friday, January 7, 1944

Darling—

Martine called to tell me that Jim Metcalfe had seen you and said how well you looked. From the reports of people who have crossed your path I've decided that you are really running a personnel bureau—and are having a perfectly wonderful time.

Last night Martine and Sandra came in the car to have dinner— while Warren came out on the bus. I couldn't help but catch my breath when I saw him get off the bus and walk toward the house—made me wonder how long it must be before I can look out and see my own man coming home once more to me. What a beautiful day that will be.

All my love,
Ann

Ann to Colie

Nashville
Tuesday, January 11, 1944

Darling—

We have run a story about you in the paper—they all jumped on me until I finally told Jack Nye to go on and use his own discretion about it—which he did. He simply said you were somewhere in Italy with the AMG and garnished it up a bit. I think you would have been pleased—Grandpa has been busy saying you should be in the paper all the time and says if I won't give out the information, he will—which worries me a little.

Devotedly,
Ann

Colie to Ann

Italy
Thursday, January 13, 1944

My dearest—

I purchased some gloves today, and want to get them off without great delay. Subject to fit, I have earmarked them as follows:

Long white ones for you. Black dress gloves with a medium length gauntlet for you. I think they are doeskin. Two pair of doeskin gloves, one white and one mauve for your mother and for Sister.

Five other pair for Josephine, Jane, Mrs. Evans, Miss Lowry, and Miss Anderson. Three pair of knit gloves for Mort, Sam, and Rob. I got a pair just like them for myself.

All of them came from a well-known manufacturer who has sold to Saks, Gimbels, and other stores for years.

Devotedly,
Colie

Colie to Ann

Italy
Saturday, January 15, 1944

My dearest—

Sometimes there are so many moving figures casting shadows of constant variety, and so much changing scenery on the stage, that one loses the sharp, distinct outline of the real characters in the play. Then, suddenly the scenery fades back, the minor players drift away, and the figure and voice, the face and being of one player contains all the intense drama of the stage. I have seen so much drama, events have crowded in so fully and swiftly, that the deep emotion in my heart has been held back. But tonight I can see no one but you, hear no voice but yours. Everywhere I turn you are there. You know that you are always in my heart and mind, but this evening you have been in this room and I have felt your hand in mine. I had to write you a love letter to tell you how wonderful you are. Neither words nor kisses alone can tell you how much I love you, but the beauty of life is the memory of our shared happiness and the anticipation of the future with you.

I love you,
Colie

Colie to Ann

Italy
Wednesday, January 19, 1944

My dearest—

You can imagine my pleasure in having Harry with me. His glow of enthusiasm remains constant, his avid pace never checked. He is a great character study, too. He never wastes a moment on nonessentials. He sleeps in his underwear, wakes up and reaches for a cigarette, is at once ready for conversation, would eat a chocolate bar as readily as a steak for breakfast (or say nothing at all if there were no breakfast), is dressed in a moment and on the go. I wore my trench coat over full uniform and heavy undershirt—his one concession to winter is a cotton undershirt, which he does not wear in the summer. I am certain he would prefer to sit on the hillside in a rainstorm with a good conversation going than to pass dull days in the greatest of luxury. His visits have pleased me mightily—he remarked on how pleasant it was to continue to cross paths and experiences. That is the one good thing of wartime, I believe.

Devotedly,
Colie

"Accompanied Col. Kincaid and Capt. Allan Shivers to scene of execution of [two spies]," Colie noted in his journal on January 21. He reported that "neither correspondents nor photographers attended the execution. Captain Harwell attended for 5th Army PRO as well as for AMG 5th Army PRO." Though he wrote his report matter-of-factly, the detail with which he wrote indicates the emotion which the deaths of these two young men must have engendered in him.

Colie to Clurie

Italy
Saturday, January 22, 1944

My dearest Clurie—

I had a letter from Grandmother today saying that you had put together a map of the world on the dining room table and that she had shown you where Italy was.

Italy looks like a big boot, doesn't it? That is, it looks like that on the map, but of course the country is so big you wouldn't ever realize its shape just by seeing it. It is as though you looked on the map and see that Tennessee is shaped like a box, but of course you wouldn't tell that except on a map.

When you live in Italy for a time, as I have, you realize that it is really not so different from home. Of course the language is different, but even on the radio you hear Italian spoken. Some of it I understand rather well, but some of it is harder to understand. But pretty soon you become accustomed to it and it seems very natural.

For instance, a minute or two ago I wanted a glass of water and I called our maid, Assunta, and asked her: "Un bicchiere d'acqua, per favore." And when she brought it, I said, "Grazie," and she answered, "Prego." That means: "A glass of water, please." Then I said, "Thanks (or thank you)" and she replied, "You're welcome."

I have showed Assunta the pictures of you and Carolyn with Mummy and she is very interested in knowing about you. She is a nice little old woman and always smiles and works very hard. I hear that she is having a romance with the funny old doorman of this apartment building and that they are going to be married. They will make a cute pair.

They have automobiles and taxis and buses over here just as we have them at home. They have beautiful houses and nice stores and the people are of all kinds: old and middle-aged and young. The children are very cute and whenever I see some of them playing I think of you and Carolyn. A number of their buildings have been damaged by the war, but they are busy cleaning things up so you don't notice them so much.

The policemen here are called *carabinieri*. They wear fancy costumes, with black coats, trousers, and black boots, and all are trimmed in brass. They are fine policemen and salute every time an Army officer passes.

I am proud of you and love you very much.

Devotedly,
Daddy

Ann to Colie

Nashville
Sunday, January 23, 1944

Darling—

My heart skipped several beats when I read about the landing only sixteen miles from Rome. I do hope we can manage to take Rome without causing too much damage. It would be dreadful to have to actually fight in the city. I've thought so much of Italy now that you are there and tried to remember the way the country looks and the feeling of it. I remember getting up early to see the entrance into Naples by boat when I took that cruise after college—I remember the summer on tour with Miss Margaret when we covered almost the entire country from the Alps on south. It was so beautiful—I wonder how it would look to me now.

Carolyn is developing into a wonderfully sweet person. As Mother says, she is so folksy—makes you feel when you come in that she is glad to see you—tells you what has gone on and wants to know what you have been doing. Yesterday Clurie went to a party and Carolyn and I walked over to Grandpa's and back—she rode the trike most of the way—she loved having the wind blow her hair and kept saying, "This is a fun day."

I have given Clurie a shelf in the library for her books and she is delighted. She has just showed me one called *Growing Up* and says it is her favorite—it is one of those that gives all the facts of life—she just showed me a picture of an egg—with the caption "This egg is ten times larger than the one you grew from." Her remark was, "That's crazy."

All my love,
Ann

Ann to Colie

Nashville
Thursday, January 27, 1943

Darling—

It seems to me that this war is bringing out more of the real values—those of us left behind have an acute realization of what we have given up—to me there will never again be anything as important as my own family circle. Our real strength will lie in the mutual interdependence of the four of us. When Carolyn prays at night and says, "Please, please God, make the war be over," then I realize that it is hard not only on me but on them to have their daddy away. I don't know why I go into all this—when I'm sure you realize much better than I what I am trying to say. Perhaps it is just that out of my own loneliness I have come better to understand what others are thinking and feeling. My own need for you is so acute—there are many days when I wonder where the strength will come from to go on to the next job, the next day. All my courage comes from the knowledge that you are thinking of me and that this will not go on forever. Without the warmth of your love behind me, I should be a complete failure—the burning desire of my life is for that day when you will once more be home.

I love you,
Ann

Ann to Colie

Nashville
Friday, January 28, 1944

Darling—

I came home late from Thayer to find your box from Sicily, a treasure trove. I'm enchanted with the carts. We ate dinner with them in the center of the table. They are going in the secretary as my most choice treasures—and the tea set is charming—I'm already looking for an opportunity to use it. The girls are thrilled with their gifts—as a special concession Clurie is being allowed to put her doll to bed in her room but only for tonight—tomorrow both dolls go in the secretary. The dresses are so quaint and cute—we are going to try them on in a few minutes—and the books—they have already divided them up and I'm sure I shall have trouble getting Clurie and Carolyn to part with any—I see now I shall have to take up Italian. The handkerchiefs are lovely—It has been a long time since I have seen linen like that. I can't tell you how much joy your presents have already given us—The carts are so festive—and imagine having the little figures in them—even to the keg of wine—and the cockades on the horses.

All my love,
Ann

Colie to Ann

Italy
Sunday, January 30, 1944

My dearest—

I miss you so much, sometimes it seems I can do nothing else. But your love is my strength. Always.

Devotedly,
Colie

CHAPTER THIRTEEN

News from Italy

Ann to Colie

Nashville

Wednesday, February 2, 1944

Darling—

Clurie is rather difficult these days—I tell her not to do something and then as soon as my back is turned she does it—Mother can do nothing with either of them—so it puts a heavy load on me. I've begun to realize—as do the psychiatrists and pediatricians now—that the old method of giving the head and not punishing just won't work.

We are still reveling in the things from Sicily. Sunday night Ann Light, Lucy, the McNeills, and the Sam Harwells came over for supper—and we had the little carts in the center of the table.

When the box arrived, Archie brought it upstairs and with much excitement we began to open it—he stood around and I finally said, "Archie, there is no sense in your acting like you are going downstairs when you know you are dying to see what is inside." So he laughed and watched the entire proceedings. What fun we had.

All my love,

Ann

Ann to Colie

Nashville

Thursday, February 3, 1944

Darling—

My mind is clouded these days with all that must be done this month and the next. Jane is handling the women's division of the Red Cross drive and I am getting 150 women for the various spots—it is a much bigger job than I had anticipated. Maggie Sloan is my assistant and is a wonderful help.

Our own Junior League advance sale starts next week—in addition to the routine Junior League business which piles up in the spring. And of course my Gray Lady work—which I love and would never under any circumstances consider a burden.

Tonight when Carolyn got in bed she didn't want to say her prayers—and I said, "Surely you want to ask God to take care of Daddy." Then she started and just before closing said, "Please, please God don't kill my Daddy—let Mummy's own husband come back."

All my love,

Ann

Colie to Ann

Italy

Monday, February 7, 1944

My dearest—

Al and I went movie-ing tonight—saw Joan Crawford in *Reunion in Paris*—probably old, but a good spy mystery.

Al is of the Austin Company, one of the great engineering-industrial construction companies. Personality contrast—he is an accomplished mouth organist [harmonica player] and has acquired three here. His music is quite cheery and his specialities are Italian numbers, "Veni Sul Mare," "Funicular," and the current Italian war hit, "Lili Marlene."

Sam has been my big boon in providing chocolate, and when I come out with a bar, it is looked on as a real treat. There is a countess doing some work about our place and I gave her one of Sam's packages to take to her young people the other day. She reported a great reception and said, "You have no idea what chocolate means when you haven't had any for such a time." I can understand that.

Got a letter from Doug Carruthers, who wrote a beautiful passage about you—"strikingly beautiful with her purple black [hat] and platinum hair piled, somewhat like a madonna with a lot of savoir faire, about her face—You should see her pride in those furs, a dark poem of forest magic and majesty—And the orchids, you should have heard her voice telling about it. You two so adore each other." Tell Doug my heart beat a symphony with the letter.

All my love,
Colie

Colie to Ann

Italy
Friday, February 11, 1944

Dearest—

Night before last I went to visit Carney. His outfit was opening a "club" and he asked me to come—I asked John Clarke to join with his new taxi-looking limousine, so we drove in style. The "club" was quite a nice spot with a bar furnished with such potables as are to be had, which are few, and a radio that adds some noise.

Probably the biggest incident of recent times is the arrival of the *Tennessean*, *Time*, *Newsweek*, and *Readers Digest*. For the first time in months I seem somewhat abreast of things at home as well as in other parts of the world. To be able to read news only a couple of weeks old changes your sense of touch with the world completely.

Devotedly,
Colie

Ann to Colie

Nashville
Saturday, February 12, 1944

Darling—

I can't help but be terribly concerned about the situation in Italy— I suppose when this reaches you the conditions will have changed considerably—but presently the situation below Rome sounds extremely grave. Like Clurie I am keeping my fingers crossed in the hopes that you won't get too near. Like Scarlett, I'll think about that tomorrow.

All my love,
Ann

Ann to Colie

Nashville
Friday, February 18, 1944

Dearest Colie—

Clurie was wondering tonight who she would vote for in the Presidential election—and seemed quite upset over the realization that she would have to wait until she was twenty-one years old.

Had a funny thing happen this week. I had to renew my B gas ration book—and when the tickets came in they only sent me ten for the three month period—I was mad as a wet hen—thinking of all my civic responsibilities and no gas—so I called the board and got Judge Howell on the phone—He said, "I'm going to tell Colie you don't read the newspapers. Each of those is worth five gallons." So I hung my head and retired from the field as quickly as possible—I had thought they were only good for two gallons.

Devotedly,
Ann

Colie to Ann

Italy
Saturday, February 19, 1944

My dearest—

Ken and John Clarke and I went to a movie—saw Ethel Merman in *Cabin in the Sky* and enjoyed it thoroughly—The last hour huddled about our heater, hearing good music on the radio—"Painted Doll," "Pistol Packing Mama," "Drink to Me Only With Thine Eyes"— Earlier Jimmy Durante and Bob Hope.

All my love,
Colie

Colie to Ann

Italy

Sunday, February 20, 1944

My dearest—

If I know nostaglia, I've had a touch today. There is nothing that brings home to my heart more surely than Sunday morning. You and the girls, the house and garden, the crowd gathering for church, Grandpa's for dinner, children swarming about, an afternoon question whether it will be a horseback ride, a sofa and the Philharmonic, or spadework in the garden, and then nighttime. It is now twilight; the girls have come in from a ride to the drugstore and play in the sun; now they're making an impasse in the playroom with funnies and dolls and talk; Clurie has her favorite radio program going. You are seeing if there are enough beans and salad to cover the situation. I am very much of a mind to mix a martini if there's enough dry vermouth. Your mother doubts if she will have one, but maybe a touch since it has been a busy day.

Would you say I know what nostalgia is? Now you see what it did to me. But I can't say that I regret it. I have enjoyed every moment, every thought.

Your letters about the girls are always about the most interesting of all. Next to you, I want to hear most of them. What your Mother said of Carolyn's being companionable made me so very eager to talk with her—and the wonderful story of your walk to Grandpa's and it being a "fun day."

Your devotion to them, your realization of responsibility, is so very fine—I'm sure I know better than anyone else how fortunate they are to have you as their mother. And, having been away so long and leaving my share of the responsibility to you, too, I can appreciate that even more now than before.

Devotedly,

Colie

Ann to Colie

Nashville
Thursday, February 24, 1944

Darling—

We had dinner night before last at Harding Place—they had fried chicken and Carolyn ate three pieces—Mother is always saying Carolyn is a meat eater, so now Carolyn has taken up the phrase herself and uses it on all occasions. I went over there last night after dinner to get a fuse—we had used all ours and had blown out some of the lights—so I was in dire straits. Grandpa reached in his pocket and drew out 50¢— said I was to buy fuses with it—so I would have some on hand.

All my love,
Ann

Ann to Colie

Nashville
Saturday, February 26, 1944

Darling—

I probably try to do too many things outside the home—but I know I wouldn't be happy doing only the domestic things—I had someone come in to stay with the girls while I did my shift at the hospital—then had Hortense come and spend the night while Mother and I went to Sam and Jo's for dinner—this morning after cooking breakfast I put the entire week's wash in the Bendix and hung it out—did some other laundry by hand—settled innumerable riots between Ann and Carolyn. Managed to pull myself together enough to join the widows' table at the Club for lunch—came home in the middle of the afternoon—dropped down for about fifteen minutes to catch my breath, went over to the Campbells to get Clurie where she had been spending the day, cooked supper, washed the dishes, got the girls to bed, and here I am. The rest of the week is going to be just as bad—because the Red Cross drive starts Tuesday—and I shall probably be on call the entire two weeks.

Yesterday afternoon late I stopped to look out the back window—it had been raining and the sun was out—brilliant on the

Grandpa's house on Harding Place.

orchard and the road going down to the gate in the back—it looked like any beautiful spring afternoon—and I suddenly remembered how many times you and I had stood and enjoyed that picture together—I thought, this is what hurts most of all—I shall never be able to see it in the brilliance of spring without having my heart ache—because we both love it so much. It's strange how such a simple thing can mean so much and can tear at one's heartstrings.

Always I think of you,
Ann

Colie to Ann

Italy
Monday, February 28, 1944

My dearest—

Al and Ken and a Capt. Crippen are writing and working at the big table and I've set up shop beside it (in close proximity to the heater). Assunta has just come through with a good job for dinner.

She starts off with some tasty and filling dishes, sometimes soup but often a version of Italian pasta, made up as well as she can with regular rations' limitations. Tonight it was rice with a touch of canned tomato and a milk and dried egg sauce. Very good. And she has sprung out recently with some pastry that is delicious. Last night it was close to doughnuts and tonight a good crusty sweet vanilla cake. She is in good graces at the moment and I feel well fed.

You'll be interested in a recent flying visit to Sardinia. It is a ragged, beautiful country, with snowcapped mountains and beautiful seashore. Not nearly as productive as the mainland, the country more nearly resembles coastal areas such as I've seen in other places. The people are much smaller than those on the mainland, but are bright and attractive, more, it seemed to me, than most any Italians. It was a quiet but thrilling trip for me and the change of scenery was rather vacation-like. I bought a couple of little pictures there, a type of native art that is modern in technique but a good spot of color I think you'll enjoy.

With all my heart,
Colie

CHAPTER FOURTEEN

Life and Hope

Ann to Colie

Nashville
Wednesday, March 1, 1944

Darling—

Monday night about 9:30 the phone rang. It was Mrs. Graham Hall, who was at the Round Table dinner commemorating their sixtieth anniversary—she said they missed you so much and thought of me—and she wanted to bring me the flowers which were in the center of the table. About 10:00 they arrived, got out of the car dressed in evening clothes in the pouring rain and brought in a beautiful arrangement of spring flowers. I really thought it was one of the nicest things I ever had done for me.

Devotedly,
Ann

Colie to Ann

Italy
early March, 1944

My dearest—

Our household has enlarged. We have taken on the part-time services of another maid, Tina, who helps Assunta with the chores, cleaning up and serving dinner. Now we can have guests most anytime we want without fear of a nervous collapse by Assunta. Assunta does everything from shine shoes to all the cooking on her one burner and we had quite a time keeping her from doing the laundry, too. Tina lives in the neighborhood and is much like Assunta, always smiling and eager to please—too eager, at times. The Italians are great for small services and you practically have to offend them to keep them from putting sugar in your coffee, buttering your bread, or taking off your shoes.

Colie

Colie to Ann

Italy
Thursday, March 2, 1944

My dearest—

You speak so seldom of your own welfare—how is your health? With all your activities, I hope you are not letting things run away with you and are keeping in good trim.

You wondered what I thought you'd be like when I got home (quoting Goode Davis)—You'll be beautiful as you always have been and you'll be neither older nor younger, but just the same, for it's the difference in our ages that matters and that will not have changed. Your hair will be perhaps grayer, but you know I love that. And what remains of mine will be the same, for I've noticed recently how gray it is in spots.

I have been lucky about staying well. I eat heartily, anything I can get, and quite regularly. Lots of candy, Sam's supply being a great help. But, with a minimum of exercise in recent months, my weight is constant and I feel pretty vigorous. I notice that in walking, others get tired before I do and few like such a fast pace. Harry and Don

Roberts are the only ones I've walked with who outdid me, even slightly. Imagine what I had today? A Coca-Cola. They're on sale at the PX now, three per week. And will they be welcome when the hot weather comes.

Colie

Colie to Ann

Italy
Thursday, March 2, 1944

My dearest—

You've probably read reviews of *A Bell for Adano* by John Hersey or may have read the book itself. I have seen the *New York Times* review which makes it sound interesting, so I hope you'll send me a copy, or maybe Jane and Rob would like to. I can think of nothing else to ask for, as our needs are remarkably taken care of by the PX. Some things we get weekly—cigarettes, a candy bar (maybe two if the supply is big), razor blades (of which I have quantities now), cookies if they have any on hand, gum, lifesavers. Other things are on a four weeks' basis—toothbrush, paste, shaving soap, shoe polish. Some clothing is rationed closely, such as winter underwear, but there is a good supply of shirts, underwear, etc.

I'm on my way to chores, lunch, PX, bath at the Red Cross, and to get copies of the book by Bill Mauldin, cartoonist for *Stars & Stripes* and of whom you may have read in *Time*. He has caught the spirit of the front in an individual, amazingly sharp manner.

Last night was one of the brightest in all these months. Sansome's Grotto opened its nightclub. Prior to that, Fred had a group of friends to dinner of his own devising. First, practically a genuine Manhattan cocktail. Then a delicious dinner: chicken soup, canapes of delicacies carried by Fred from New York himself, the main and amazing dish of Virginia ham under juicy chicken. Fred recalled, as he often does, your charming hospitality and said your ham was much better. He recalled our cocktail champagne party and even produced a glass of Strega after dinner, then champagne at the club gala. And what a gala! A swell orchestra and a floor show that would be at home on 52nd Street. I asked him if this was to go on every night and Fred said, "Hell, no—we'll have a different show every night!" Harry and I partook of the dancing and gaiety, walked home at midnight laughing most of the way.

All my love,
Colie

Colie to Ann

Italy
Saturday, March 4, 1944

My dearest—

Last night John Clarke entertained at dinner. There were Harry, John Ames, an attractive English girl, John, and me. John took us all up the hill (mountain would be more accurate) amid the customary laughter that travels with him. I think the young lady had to hold her breath with some of John's banter going on, but we explained that John was quite subtle and somewhat shy. John's landlord also showed up and his cook, Amelia, aided him to the table, which was topped with one of her customary splendid meals. Afterward we settled the world's problems over cognac until about 11:00.

Devotedly,
Colie

Ann to Colie

Nashville
Sunday, March 5, 1944

Darling—

You know how slow I have always been to quote other people or even to interpret for them—but I am getting almost violent these days. Perhaps it is due in part to the feeling that I have established a definite place for myself in this community and have suddenly begun to realize that people listen to me—I have always felt that you did such a beautiful job at that and my contribution was rather negligible—much to my amazement I find that I actually have a contribution of my own to make. Whereas I used to hesitate to unequivocally make a statement I now make it—with certain reservations of course—but I make it and let the chips fly where they may.

From my vantage point there are many people here who hardly know there is a war going on. There are many others who feel it strongly and are trying as best they can to make whatever contribution they can, while at the same time trying to keep life as normal as possible—which of course is vitally important. Those of us who are most affected are the ones who say the least—I don't pretend like some that everything is lovely—nor do I cry on my friends' necks as others do—but I see no reason for people to think it is easy—which it certainly is not. I feel that I contribute my full share to any gathering I am in. And I am doing all and sometimes more than I should do for the war effort and all civic enterprises—but there are some people who do nothing and of course never will.

We really don't feel the war here—those of us who have people overseas do—but the mechanics of living go on much the same—we have plenty to eat, we can still get some liquor—all the luxuries we need if we can pay for them—and so it goes.

I am already beginning to worry as to whether we are realistic enough about the peace—Russia seems to definitely have her feet on the ground—I wonder about us.

All my love,
Ann

Colie to Ann

Italy
Tuesday, March 7, 1944

My dearest—

In order to keep up with our organization's work, I recently spent time with our forward men. That meant going into towns where the Germans had been a short time before, hearing and seeing the big guns, the foxholes, trying to get food to the hungry and to begin from the bottom up the rebuilding of war's wreckage. I was eager to see and take part in it. Campbell Dickson and his two tent mates made room for my bedding roll on the ground and shared the welcome, though smelly, warmth of their kerosene stove. I had taken a bottle of cognac, and a couple of other officers came in to report then to help consume it. We went to bed somewhat warmed, but I'm afraid the whole bottle couldn't have done the job for me. They had bunks and mattress covers filled with straw. But that didn't keep the chill of the ground from penetrating. I was awake a good while before 0630, waited quietly while Dick manfully lighted the stove, then crawled out. It took my best setting-up exercises to get the blood flowing again, but then a cupful of ice water to wash and shave in set me back again.

By then it was almost light. I stepped outside—the red, orange, purple streaks of sunrise were bursting over the beautiful snow-capped ridges, the most brilliant moon you ever saw (except, perhaps, at Casablanca) was still shining, and there were beautiful stars in the sky—on the opposite hill, a clinging village looked like pure marble in the early light. In the not too great distance, there was the occasional roar of a gun—now there came a multitude of propellers in the sky—I smelled bacon cooking—it was too real to be a dream, but much too dreamlike to be reality.

In a short while, the major and I piled into a Jeep, the driver headed north. We went through some beautiful country, but there was too much going on to keep your attention focused on beauty. I was busy keeping my helmet on with one hand while I held on to the Jeep with the other. Then the driver hit a straight section of road. "I call this Messerschmidt Boulevard," he said, "hold on." I did.

We drove a long way, then saw a town in the distance that looked beautiful, pink and white and yellow. But as we dodged shell holes on the narrow, winding road, drawing closer I saw that the town was not so pretty now. The big pink building that looked like a library or college hall was windowless, the roof torn off, great holes in the outer walls, the inside a shambles. Gradually we could see that this was the case of all other buildings in the town. We drove up to the edge, dismounted, and walked up a narrow street.

All the streets were narrow. Inside the town itself there was no street built for automobiles. Most of them were really paths, with steps leading up and down.

The scene was of devastation. There was hardly a building with a roof on it. The "streets" were littered with debris, the insides of houses were wrecked. We saw no one until we came to a narrow doorway where the room was cleanly swept and a wooden partition had been put across what had been the entrance to a living room. A little boy and girl were sitting there playing. As we came in, the girl began to cry, but then her brother said something to her and she stopped. The boy came out to us and we asked him to show us the town square. He was clean and handsome and bright-eyed. He took us quickly over debris and through streets on which hollow-eyed houses looked out, to the little piazza, where a few people were gathered. We talked to them and were told about how many people there were in town. They had a little food—there was only one case of bad sickness.

The town priest and secretary told what they knew of conditions. They and our officers estimated how much food was needed immediately. As we walked out on the other side of town, we found an old woman who had been too sick to take to the hills. Neighbors were taking care of her. We found a German's body still in a doorway, told some men to bury him that afternoon. In one battered corner building was a German machine gun, with shells scattered all about it. Just across the street, several women were cleaning up their homes.

The next day we went back to that town with the first shipment of food. Many more people were there, having come from their hiding places in the hills. The priest stood in the piazza talking with us about caring for the people. The secretary had his overcoat thrown over his shoulders. He took inventory of the food stock, locked it carefully in a cage next to the barber shop—The barber had done the best job of cleaning up his place. It made an unreal contrast, standing clean though windowless—the barber was very attentively shaving a customer. (What would you expect a barber to be doing, I reflected.)

Two women were standing in a portico as bombs dropped near enough to whistle. The younger woman went inside her house to cry, the older one stood and listened to the conversation she couldn't understand and the crying she couldn't do anything about. A little boy was sweeping debris from an upstairs office where administration was to begin. Later he was sweeping up the premises where a bakery was being set up to make bread—A bright woman with a Scottish burr was showing us the bakery, of which she was in charge—There were two young mothers with babies in their arms—Indeed there was life and hope. There must always be hope when home means so much to people that they will bring back from a shambles the home that is in their hearts, and there establish it once again.

Devotedly,
Colie

CHAPTER FIFTEEN

A New Assignment

In March, Colie became a Civil Affairs Officer, assigned to British Eighth Army.

Ann to Colie

Nashville
Saturday, March 11, 1944

Darling—

Mother ordered some new roses to go in the garden and has been out today watering them until she can get them in the ground and wishing as she did all last summer for the services of a strong man to get the place in shape—then when she begins to realize that is hopeless, she says she wishes she had the strength to do it herself.

I love you,
Ann

Colie to Ann

Italy
Tuesday, March 14, 1944

My dearest—

My current boss is an amusing and engaging character, one Capt. Carl Bischoff, who talks, eats, acts, and thinks like Lum, or it may be Abner. One of the luxuries of this place is a two-minute walk to the office and a radio therein. *Stars & Stripes* is a bit more difficult to obtain than at times in the past, so radio reports are big events. Dependence on the radio whets the appetite for written news; and, if there was ever doubt of written dominance, it seems to me this war would have resolved it, for the demand is constant for papers, magazines, books.

Goodnight for this night and, as for every other one, my great and constant love.

Devotedly,
Colie

In the following letter, Colie speaks to Ann of their wedding anniversary. They were married in Columbia, Tennessee, on March 29, 1932.

Colie to Ann

Italy
Wednesday, March 15, 1944

My dearest—

If I were there on the 29th of March, I know how we would enjoy talking about that day—I remember every detail. Driving in style to Columbia on the prettiest spring day that ever dawned in glorious Tennessee—the busy time before church—the reception and photographers—whisking away in George's car—then the first part of a ride that led to such great happiness that no one event can stand as reminder of it all.

Devotedly,
Colie

The wedding of Ann McLemore and Coleman Harwell, March 29, 1932. Front row, left to right: Jane McKelvey, Julia Clements Brooks, Ann and Coleman Harwell, Virginia Orr Watkins, Emma Childers Derryberry. Back row, left to right: Rob Harwell, Dwight Webb, Robert Brandau, Briggs McLemore Jr., Dr. George Williamson, Morton Howell, Louis Johnson, Paul Derryberry, Sam Harwell Jr.

Ann to Colie

Nashville
Monday, March 20 and
Tuesday, March 21, 1944

My darling—

The Red Cross, at least my part of it, is finished—and we went almost $300 over our quota—I've been heading for town at 8:30 each morning—so you can imagine my relief at being able to call some of my time my own. Mother celebrated by going to Columbia Saturday.

Sometimes time and the war drag so I feel this "interlude" will never pass—Then I feel that I have no right to complain—

remembering your letter about the visit to the front—I realize that each day I should thank God for what I have—and yet no prayer of thankfulness can be fully heartfelt until you are a part of it.

Hortense stayed with the girls last night—I went to the Wilsons for dinner—and when I left, Hortense and Clurie were busy doing string tricks—I heard Clurie say earlier, "Come on Hortense. Let's go get some supper." They were a cute pair. Hortense has developed a sudden devotion to me—which touches me deeply—I'm extremely fond of her—

Ann

Ann to Colie

Nashville
Thursday, March 23, 1944

Darling—

The person who gets things done in this family is Grandpa—he took this typewriter in for me this morning at eleven o'clock—it is now only a little after three and he has already returned it fixed.

The fruit trees are in full bloom in the orchard and are beautiful—Rob says I should sow the orchard in some sort of grass—so I suppose I shall have to arrange that.

Sunday is our annual open house at the Junior League Home and the following Sunday is the day of the paper sale. Then June 1, I turn the reins over to someone else—and I will be glad. I shall probably miss the feeling of having my hand on the rudder but it will be good to attend to my own business instead of spending all my time on someone else's. You asked me about myself—I'm eating and sleeping well—still thin—but had myself gone over about a month ago and was in good shape—I'm doing too much what with home duties and civic affairs—but if I'm not busy I think too much and that is no good—I'm going to try some way to go off for about a week on my own just to ease this burden of responsibility a little.

Devotedly,
Ann

Colie to Ann

Italy
Sunday, March 26, 1944

My dearest—

It is the end of a comparatively uneventful Sunday. Two colleagues are before the fireplace reading and listening to the radio. I have the use of the dining-living room table, as our other colleague and chief, Maj. Harris, has hit the hay early. These are pleasant surroundings; our living-dining room is small, but it has the three items you could most desire under these conditions: a good light, an open fire, and a radio (we've had the town electrician put it in shape and tonight it has brought in BBC news and Mr. Churchill's speech). And, always a top item, we eat well. We are fortunate to have a former chef who produces some appetizing items, as tonight when dessert was a big slice of cake with chocolate topping.

We have two boys to round out the home staff. They are both very bright. The larger, Pepino Grande, is a former tailor and was clever enough to save me a pair of trousers today by fixing the zipper. The other, Pepino Piccolo, is a black-haired, black-eyed, red-cheeked youngster of fifteen, who belies any of the hardships that he must have seen.

Our living room is the place of gathering, as our only heat is here, but it is cozy and we have a good pool of magazines and books. I share a bedroom with a lieutenant, a very solid young fellow from Chicago. Having a canvas bed, I was lucky to find a mattress to go on top of it. The feature of our living quarters that we are fortunate to have but that requires the greatest fortitude is a balcony toilet. I would gladly swap its beautiful view via paneless window for some steam heat, but I realize that is a very small attitude to take.

I have thought of you and the girls so much today. Sunday is always the day that brings you closest to me.

Devotedly,
Colie

Colie to Ann

Italy
Tuesday, March 28, 1944

My dearest—

I wonder how your problems are developing these days—Has Archie departed from the fold? How does the garden grow and is Mr. O'Brien still in charge of your sharecropper project? Have you a cook and do you have to do all the home laundry on the Bendix? Are you going to be able to get that trip away? I see by the paper that the garden program is on again, and I'm thinking of that good soil and wishing I were able to give you my usually invaluable aid in tilling it. Did the grass seed produce?

It is hard to realize how long I have been away from you. Somehow, this life becomes less strange as the months carry on. Keeping you constantly in my thoughts, having your wonderful letters coming to me in a steady stream, has taken you with me in my thoughts wherever I've gone. And I have the feeling that the things that once were so strange and that now seem so matter-of-fact to me, must seem the same to you. Funny-looking Pepino Grande, with his tousled hair and growing-boy-disheveled way, just popped in to borrow some fire for their quarters and I asked him to replenish the *aqua potabile* supply—his "guda night" and my "buona notte" seem very usual—it doesn't seem strange to find myself suddenly tired of a German radio program and then to shut it off—all the conglomeration of news fiction characters and things I see every day have come to be as normal as Church Street or Broadway—and it doesn't seem possible that they could appear otherwise to you, for you have seen them with me day after day. Of course I must remind myself that this has been in my mind, since much that I would tell you must go unsaid—Today, for instance, I was looking at some beautiful postcards I had bought and thinking of the day I would show them to you and tell you what they have meant to me, and that too became a part of my thinking, as though I had already shown them to you and you had asked questions and said we must plan a trip to Italy to see all these people and places—It is well that I think this way. It would be much more difficult if I did not feel that you shared my life, as I want you to do and as I know you want to do—So, after twelve years of the greatest happiness any person ever brought another, that is the way you have become a constant part of my living.

Your devoted,
Colie

Ann to Colie

Nashville
Thursday, March 30, 1944

Darling—

I'm keeping my fingers crossed these days and talking little about my domestic situation which has taken a nice turn for the better. Monday my little girl from Murfreesboro brought back with her a friend who is doing the laundry, upstairs work, and looking after Carolyn. It is a joy to have someone around who tries to do things the way you want and is young and energetic. I didn't write you but I have been worn out from doing so much myself—I've been doing everything from the laundry to firing the furnace—so while this beautiful dream lasts I'm trying to collect myself—and if it continues I may even play an occasional game of golf.

Everytime the phone rings at night we get excited thinking it might be Briggs—I am going to give a real party for him when he comes—It would be wonderful if you were both going to be here—or better still I'll settle for having you home—you've no idea how much I dream of just that.

Devotedly,
Ann

On March 29, Colie wrote in his journal about his and Ann's wedding anniversary:

I have thought a great deal of my happiness in these years, and have been continually thankful for the deep and joyous memories they have given me. No part of it is more satisfying than this, when, taken away from my beloved wife and children, my home and many dear ones, I can live tranquilly and confident of love.

Then, too, there is my constant sense of companionship with Ann. In every moment of relaxation, of contemplation—in the presence of beauty such as the mountain waterfall and winding stream—in the narrow winding streets where every figure strikes emotion's chords—in all of these she is my constant companion. I know her laughter and her tears. They are always mine—as unobtrusive, as poignant, as they have become in these twelve years of fruitful life together.

Today I heard of the deaths of two colleagues. Not men I had known, but two in whose footsteps I am following. My thought at once was of their wives and homes. And of my own. In such a time one struggles silently with fear.

Foolish to have chosen this more hazardous road? Never—there are dangers as great on the others, and not to have chosen it would have been to deny responsibility and honor and self-esteem. Here is the work I have trained for and sought, here is my reason for these months and miles that separate me from those so much in my heart tonight. And there are other roads ahead—mud and mines and devastation. Others are on it tonight—those big guns still seem very far away. No glamour, but satisfaction.

And that marks twelve years. God bless my beautiful, wise, courageous Ann, and our two lovely daughters. May I be always in their heart and they in mine.

Colie to Ann

Italy
Friday, March 31, 1944

My dearest—

I find myself enjoying very pleasant companionship. There are four of us living together. Dill, a great, bulging Red Crosser, is from Washington. At first he struck me as being rather abrupt and not too companionable. Now I find he is companionship itself, will talk twenty-four hours a day, is extremely considerate. Younger Carl Anderson is formerly of the Chicago police, an intelligent, straight-forward fellow who knows how to get things done. Then there is Major Harris, former Minneapolis city official, a cleancut and forceful fellow. We live a businesslike life, shoptalk and personal talk flow together and it's rather hard to tell where business ends and personal matters begin.

One of the things I have always enjoyed has been that AMG brings you in close contact with British as well as Americans. In many circumstances, you lose sight of which they are and they're just people. I'm glad to have made several warm friends among the British.

Today the Major had to be away from the office, so he put me in charge. There couldn't have been a more interesting day for it. Problems that arise about food supplies and work details, all the things that make up small town life. And such a conglomeration of languages—our secretary (male), a delightful youngster who has six years of university experience, speaks French fluently and is outdoing my Italian with his English. I start a sentence in English and conclude in Italian, or vice versa. Sometimes people come in who speak neither, then we have practically a sign language test. Much saluting and heel clicking and much that is plain courtesy and manners.

The Italians never let me through a day without a new surprise. Like the little fellow who opens the door quietly and bows nearly to the floor and whispers, "Per-mayso," and then slips in and draws up his full five feet with a click of the heels and head tilted on one side.

And the weezened old woman with a hill dialect that no one of us could make a thing out of. And the four women who were well dressed, the oldest with a fur collared coat, and who came in surrounded by half a dozen children underfoot, including two little black-eyed girls with apple cheeks and a sparkling-eyed little boy who half whistled all the time and squinted his eyes at me.

Maybe you have the idea that I like it. Well, I'm rather guilty of that, I guess. It is hard work, but it concerns human beings who are tremendously responsive and, I believe, appreciative. A thing I like most is expressed in the advice an older officer gave me a long while ago, "Never do for the Italians what you can make them do for themselves." And I see many evidences of their doing things for themselves. Most of all I like that.

If I had time, I would feel sorry for those who do not see the things I see. I wouldn't trade my work and my experiences for any I have known.

I hope you know how constantly you are in my thoughts—tell Clurie and Carolyn that a day never passes I do not think of them many times and that every night they are in my prayers.

With all my heart,
Colie

CHAPTER SIXTEEN

Grandpa's Birthday

Ann to Colie

Nashville
Saturday, April 1, 1944

Darling—

With no apparent warning the bus drivers went on strike yesterday—this place is quiet with no traffic on the road in front of us. They are striking for a wage increase—but the procedure is termed an unauthorized strike. The place is tied in knots.

At 3 A.M. this morning the phone rang and it was Briggs calling from San Francisco. He is going to New York to make his report and then come on here.

Devotedly,
Ann

Colie to Ann

Italy
Sunday, April 2, 1944

My dearest—

Your letter about people and the war was particularly interesting. You have always had an audience and your counsel has been wise and respected. Not least in factors bearing on this has been that you weren't too free with your views nor are you contentious. But sane and soundly spoken, rather than gushy or set in rock, both of which apply to some people.

All my love,
Colie

Ann to Colie

Nashville
Monday, April 3, 1944

Darling—

The Junior League paper sale yesterday came off in great style in spite of rain—we were hitting for $50,000—and made $60,000.

Last night I had dinner at the Nyes. The McNicholases and the Evanses were there—Mr. Evans was celebrating his fiftieth birthday. He talked a lot about you to me—how much he thought of you and how proud he was of you and how your place when you returned was to take over the paper again, etc.—all very flattering—you would have enjoyed it.

The bus strike is over—they started running again this morning—which was a great relief to all—the case has not been settled but goes to the WLB for discussion—meanwhile we can still get around. And with only two gallons of gas a week, it was just in time.

You seem so far away from me tonight. I feel that you have been away for years. Carolyn said tonight that when you came home she was going to get you to help her make some curtains for the dollhouse—and then she would clean it all up and have it ready when company came.

You are in my heart always—
Ann

Colie to Anne Williamson McLemore

Italy
Tuesday, April 4, 1944

Dearest Mother Mac—

This is beautiful country, an extremely interesting place full of interesting characters. No place in the world could fascinate me more, nor give me greater enthusiasm for my work. And enthusiasm for work is mighty important to me now, for being away from home would be rough without it.

I have not heard in a while about Briggs' status and naturally am very much interested. I certainly hope it has not been necessary for him to come home from doing such an important job. Should he come, however, I believe he will find much compensation. There is a lot to be said for playing your shots as they're called and, even where it seems unfortunate for a man to shift from a position in which he is so fully capable, still he can be gratified by doing a good job wherever Uncle Sam needs or puts him. That may seem muddled philosophy, but it adds up to one that we as a nation have to take. I know that Briggs will get along splendidly and do a fine job wherever he is and whatever he's doing.

I can never tell you how much it means to me for you to be with Ann and the girls. Her letters continually reflect her gratitude and I want you to know of mine, too.

With devoted love,
Colie

Ann to Colie

Nashville
Wednesday, April 5, 1944

Darling—

Your box arrived from Italy—what a treasure hunt—everything arrived in perfect shape—the gloves are gorgeous—I haven't seen any so lovely since the war started—the white ones you chose for me are perfect—the black ones are a bit large so I took a beige pair instead—because the beige ones will go with my Easter outfit—also because I couldn't resist the pearl buttons on them. The little boxes for Marie and Nancy and Mortie came out first and I was simply holding my breath for fear there would not be one for me—and mine is by far the most delightful—I have loved those boxes ever since I saw them in Sorrento years ago. The pin is lovely—I've always loved coral—and this one is so delicate and lovely. Grandpa was quite touched by your tie—thought it was beautiful and said you had been keeping him in ties for twenty years. The Robert Harwells were delighted with their things. I took the boxes to Marie when I took Grandpa his tie—she was delighted with hers and with your remembering Mortie and Nancy—Mother is delighted with her gloves and with the bracelet. I like my things best of all—you have shown such superb taste in all your purchases. And I'm having a wonderful time with them.

Devotedly,
Ann

Ann to Colie

Nashville
Thursday, April 6, 1944

Darling—

They have made Grandpa a bedroom downstairs after all these years and he is apparently happy as a lark—though this is his first night in it and he may change his mind tomorrow—They have moved everything out of the dining room and brought his big bed down. When I called Mort a few minutes ago to see how it was setting with him, he said Grandpa had already gone to bed and said he never expected to go upstairs any more. I know you would be glad to hear it and to know he no longer had to negotiate the stairs. Mother is really responsible—but nobody knows it—certainly not Grandpa.

Jane just called to tell me that Rob had gotten a man who will drive Grandpa and act as nurse-companion—to Grandpa they will call him a chauffeur—but he will nevertheless be there to look after him when Mort and Marie are away at night. We are all planning a big celebration next week when he will be eighty years old.

Clurie and Carolyn are still talking about the trip to Charlottesville—they remember every detail—and when other children talk about their daddies being home—Clurie goes back to that trip with pride in her voice and tells about it. It was wonderful that they were with us—it gives them something to hold to.

Devotedly,
Ann

Colie to Ann

Italy
Friday, April 7, 1944

My dearest—

This was Good Friday, a big day in Italy. Easter seems to take on greater meaning here and inspire greater festivity than in America. They make more of it than Christmas—today there was the big procession of the *Gesu Morto* (Dead Jesus)—a citywide occasion. Special permission was given to hold the parade and we marched in it to show respect—It is, in fact, a funeral procession led by several hooded figures of mourners carrying crosses—one or two carrying busts of Jesus—then pallbearers carrying a white litter upon which rests the lifesize figure of Jesus, fully realistic. Then the hierarchy, followed by a lifesize standing figure of the Virgin Mary. A strange aspect of the parade is that money is pinned to the robes of the Virgin. It is handed or thrown from balconies or windows to the marchers, who then pin the bill received to those already attached. Before the parade was over, there were several long strands of money.

Behind the priests were some soldiers, then a group of little girls and Sisters from the local orphanage. They all wear little black round hats (like tams) and capes to match. The Sisters led them continuously in prayers and they responded—there was a band playing a funeral dirge, and between band music there were male and female choirs—The march was through the length of the town and everyone was out to witness it. The tears are copious. Especially among the old women, who look toward the figure of Christ as though He were actually there. You can imagine the effect of the funeral music and the tears—with this town as a background, it was one of the most dramatic events I have ever witnessed.

Devotedly,
Colie

Ann to Colie

Nashville
Sunday, April 9, 1944

Darling—

It's Easter Sunday—the children have been up since daylight. I believe they have enjoyed it more than Christmas—they had big

bunnies by their beds and eggs all over the house—and I could hear Clurie wandering around in the early hours exclaiming over the eggs—just as I would be about to go back to sleep one or the other would come in with something to show me. They also have two live chicks and two chickens, which they adore and spend most of their time with. I got them to Sunday School by the hardest and when Mother, Mildred Nielsen, and I finally arrived at church, there was not a seat in the place and we sat on the steps in the balcony.

Coleman Harwell, April 1944.

Ann

Ann to Colie

Nashville
Tuesday, April 11, 1944

Darling—

I have made a discovery—if we had a different dining room table our room would look a great deal larger. I had a chance to buy a beauty for $250—but couldn't quite see it in these times. I'm afraid we are going to have to make some repairs on our driveway—we are getting some deep holes in it which stay filled with water. Do you think I should go ahead and have it fixed or what? I don't like to let things run down too much—don't think it wise.

This talk must sound trivial to you—but it goes into keeping up the morale—It is the everyday problems that have kept me from going nuts—If I hadn't had my outside activities and inside problems I would be a pretty sorry sight. This whole war is much too close to me for comfort—and lack of activity leads to brooding.

Devotedly,
Ann

Robert E. Harwell to Colie

Nashville
Tuesday, April 11, 1944

Dear Colie—

Father has been upset in the last two weeks, so I got his promise to let Dr. Owsley Manier come to see him. Owsley found that he had the same trouble with his heart that he had before, but he does not regard it as anything serious. As a matter of fact, Father started on his treatment which Dr. Manier gave him, had a fine night, and reported that he was much better. He is up the entire time enjoying his red chair, but as yet he has not been to the store.

We were also fortunate to get a young man from the Seventh Day Adventists recommended by Mr. Hilgers, a friend of ours at the Madison Sanitarium. Father must be well pleased with him, for he is calling him Tommy.

I trust that everything continues to go along well for you and that you are still well and satisfied with your work.

Jane, Robin, Jonny, and Coleman, I am sure, will want to join me in this letter with much love.

Devotedly,
Rob

Ann to Colie

Nashville
Sunday, April 16, 1944

Darling—

The girls and Mother have gone for a ride with Grandpa. I think he is enjoying having his driver—he has taken the children to get ice cream almost every day this week.

Devotedly,
Ann

Colie to Clurie

Italy
Sunday, April 16, 1944

My Darling Clurie—

I hope this letter reaches you in time for your birthday. If I were there, I would join Mummy, Grandmother, and Carolyn in singing "Happy Birthday" to you. I remember singing it to you before and I still have a picture of you that I snapped when you were two years old and you were smiling at the cake with two candles on it. And now you will have a cake with eight candles!

I mailed a package to Mummy with presents for you and Carolyn. Your present is a handmade Italian rag doll, a long-legged girl with hair in braids and dressed like Italian country girls do.

Tell Carolyn I have sent her a present, too, and will write her a birthday letter, too.

I am very proud of you and love you very much.

Your devoted,
Daddy

Ann to Colie

Nashville
Monday, April 17, 1944

Darling—

The girls are busy planning their birthdays—I've tried to talk Clurie into having a movie party but she wants to have something at home. Then we will have Carolyn's birthday and she has already told me that she wants two cakes with pink icing and candles. I told her she could not have two and she said, well all right, but the one she had would have to be very, very big. Also she said she did not want any clothes for a present but wanted something to play with. They are so positive—particularly Clurie who has gotten to the stage of arguing about everything. You should be here—I run out of words after a certain length of time.

Ann

Samuel K. Harwell Sr. to Colie

Nashville
Thursday, April 20, 1944

Dear Coleman—

We had a great occasion yesterday. I celebrated my eightieth birthday. I had all of my children except you, and all of the grandchildren with me. You were remembered and many times spoken of.

I see lots of your family, Ann, Mrs. McLemore, and the little girls. The little girls are very charming and seem to be living a very happy life. They come over to my house every day or two and quite frequently have meals with us.

We often wonder what you are doing but we know that it is impossible for you to tell us.

Your home looks very beautiful now. I think they are gardening over there and planting a lot of vegetables as well as planting some flowers.

I frequently take your family out for a little drive, as much as my gasoline will permit.

Be sure and take good care of yourself and keep well and strong.

I will be mighty glad when we have won the war and have suitable peace again.

I remain your devoted,
Father

Sam K. Harwell Sr. with five of his grandchildren: Evalina, Leila, Clurie, Robin, and Sambo.

Ann to Colie

Nashville
Thursday, April 20, 1944

Darling—

Yesterday Grandpa celebrated his eightieth birthday—and wore your Italian tie very proudly. All the family as well as the Keelings and Mr. Martin dropped by and had ice cream and cake. The store had sent him a beautiful three-tier cake—then there were other cakes and the children had a wonderful time eating all they wanted. Even baby Coleman was on hand—Grandpa looks much better—I believe he has gotten off a little weight—they have him on a diet again and when we arrived he was sitting on the porch—so all goes well.

The gas situation is getting so tight here that when I ran the hookup this morning I left my car at H. G. Hills [grocery]—came back home on the bus—then will catch the bus here, pick up the car, and get the children—all of which maneuvering will save me about half a gallon of gas. I've never been so thankful for anything as I am for being on the bus line.

All my love,
Ann

Colie to Ann

Italy
Thursday, April 20, 1944

My dearest—

I'm delighted to hear that Briggs is back. It is amazing to realize what distances we have covered between us. Once it used to startle me to hear some British friend say casually that he'd been away from home three or four years, or had seen a brother for the first time in five or ten years. Now I get some idea of that. Not that I anticipate such a term for myself, but I know that I've been away from Nashville a year now and separated from you nine months. Nine months that have been full of heartaches and longing, but tempered and made bearable by sweet memories, wonderment, and activity.

I've been trying to get some fishing tackle because the streams about us are terribly inviting. An afternoon along one of the banks would be well spent, even though no fish were in sight. It is a strange picture that men can take an afternoon off from war to fish.

This is a plain building and would rate as new in this part of the world. We have four rooms surrounding the stairway hall. One of them has a fireplace and is our dining-living room. It was formerly a kitchen and has a sink in one corner under which our firewood is stacked. There are three comfortable chairs about a fireplace and a little love seat that matches two of the chairs. There is a long, hard sofa across the room that serves as a hat throw, an arm chair with a soft seat, five straight chairs. There is also a twenty litre, straw wrapped wine cask that we keep filled, with some difficulty, for dinner use. A rather continual overflow of visitors taps our supplies heavily.

On the floor above us our enlisted men live, surrounded by two families of nine and eleven members each. I don't see much of the families, except a rather constant flow of children up and down. One of them (the eleven member unit) have their living room in our kitchen and use the same stove. Most of them are out all day working and as they have only one heavy meal a day at home, it is workable, though I think the stove is taxed.

My own room is the same size as our living room and sometimes is shared, sometimes used by me alone. I use my army canvas cot which is covered with a mattress. No sheets. I have a mattress cover which I use for a couple of weeks; then, while I'm having it washed, I sleep between the blankets. I have the blankets thoroughly aired at least every week. The other furnishings are the ever present Italian bedside table, half of a round table in one corner supporting a large mirror, a bookcase used for a dresser, and a type of Italian Grand Rapids dressing table. Then there are two chairs. No wall decor, the usual stone floor found in a country where stone is much cheaper than wood. The little dresser is lined with my pictures so I feel much at home.

I am pleased to have my own motor and driver. Not exactly the kind of motor you'd drive down Belle Meade Boulevard, but the kind that suits these roads much better, a one and a half ton truck. It is preferable to a Jeep, for it can be used to haul the supplies, people, or whatever, and can also serve me for all purposes. It is a perfect luxury-necessity combination for this job.

I love you with all my heart,
Colie

CHAPTER SEVENTEEN

A Quiet Passing

Telegram from Ann to Colie

Nashville,
Friday, April 21, 1944

YOUR FATHER PASSED AWAY EARLY THIS MORNING HEART ATTACK
VERY QUIETLY NO SUFFERING JUST AS HE WOULD HAVE WISHED HAD
BEEN WELL AND HAPPY FUNERAL SATY APRIL 22ND MY HEART WITH
YOU LOVE ANN UNQUOTE HEALTH AND WELFARE OTHER MEMBERS
FAMILY EXCELLENT FAMILY WILL WRITE

Ann to Colie

Nashville
Saturday, April 22, 1944

Darling—

I hate your being off in a strange land by yourself when this news
reaches you. Grandpa was so proud of what you were doing—and
although it is hard for you being so far away from the family at this
time—it seems fitting that you should be doing the job you are. Clurie
and Carolyn are taking the whole thing quite sanely—Clurie was a
little upset at first. Her first reaction was to worry about you—She

Sam Harwell Sr.

said, "I wonder what effect this will have on Daddy." You would be proud of them both. The funeral is to be today at three o'clock at home.

You are always in my heart—and I only wish I could have been with you when this came. But my spirit has been there with you continuously—you are never really alone.

Devotedly,
Ann

Colie did not receive the news of his father's death until May.

Colie to Ann

Italy
Sunday, April 23, 1944

My dearest—

I thought many times throughout this lovely day of home and the garden, fruit trees and flowers, sun and sky, and you—there was much to remind me. I saw a patch of deep purple iris and remembered that our first would be in bloom now. I saw two women in calf-deep black soil moving down the rows, seeds in one hand, a stick in the other, jabbing and sowing, covering with the stick. The land is alive. You could taste spring itself. I could feel your presence every moment.

Devotedly,
Colie

Ann to Colie

Nashville
Sunday, April 23, 1944

Darling—

Yesterday during the service I felt that it was not I there—it was you I was representing. When I stood with Marie, Sam, and Rob at the cemetery, it was not I, but you who was in my place. The day was a glorious sunshiny one and the house looked like a flower garden. Beverly Douglas and Mary Ragland sang two hymns with Martha Bartles at the piano. Dr. Ragsdale was there with Bill Phifer and prayed a beautiful prayer in which he asked that God be with you in your heart since you were far away from home. All the old servants were on hand—Hortense, Dicey, Belle, and Robert Mackey. Grandpa's going was a terrible blow to Mackey.

Never forget how much you mean to me. Your sorrows are mine—and I love you with all my heart.

Ann

Jane McKelvey Harwell to Colie

Rolling River Farm, Franklin, TN
Sunday, April 23, 1944

Dearest Colie—

There is so much we all want to say to you, to make it easier for you to bear the shock of your father's going. We tried to word the cable so you would understand how easily and peacefully the end came and what a wonderful last week he had with his family and friends, in celebration of his eightieth birthday.

I find it so hard to say what we have all been thinking these past two days every time we have thought of you. No matter how many times you have realized that this might happen, that did not ease the shock of the news. And yet you would not have done otherwise. Grandpa was so proud of what you were doing, and how happy you must be to know how much satisfaction you gave him in your lifetime. Rob quoted him so many times as saying that you had never given him any concern in your whole life.

Our dearest love to you, in which Rob and all three of our little boys join me.

Devotedly,
Janey

Jack Nye of the Tennessean wrote Colie on April 25: "It will be no surprise to know that Ann met this emergency with her accustomed courage and wisdom. I think it was especially difficult for her, but one would never have known it."

Colie to Ann

Italy
Tuesday, April 25, 1944

My dearest—

The intense quiet of this room is in sharp contrast with the hilarity above, where our enlisted men are singing "Tipperary," "M'amselle from Armentiers," and other windjammers. Now the scene shifts, as Pepino Grande comes in to ask if we need more fire and I have told him to add a bit more wood, although it is not essential. It cheers the place.

You can imagine how I'd like to be there these days, with the yard breaking forth with flowers, with everything at its peak of life. I think of every spot of the yard and orchard and garden, every room of the house, everyone I love so much, and first and always of you. Tell the girls how much I love them.

Your devoted,
Colie

Ann to Colie

Nashville
Tuesday, April 25, 1944

Darling—

Almost any day I expect to see Grandpa drive up with Coca-Colas for the girls and an offer to get some ice cream—his was such a strong personality that I think his spirit will be with us always.

The girls are having a wonderful time these days with the pigeon house—they have chairs and beds made of bricks and I believe they even have a guest room—it keeps them outdoors, too.

We now have planted in the garden turnip greens, onions, tomatoes, lettuce, and radishes. The roses are full of buds and we actually have some of our own lily of the valley.

I think of you so much, darling—don't be lonely or blue; the girls and I think and talk of you constantly—you are always with us. And everything points to the day when you will be back.

All my love,
Ann

Sam K. Harwell Jr. to Colie

Nashville
Thursday, April 27, 1944

Dear Colie—

If only you could have been here to see the magnificent display of love and affection which came from all sides—from people, many of whom we hardly knew, whose lives had been touched by Father's generosity during the years of the past.

I only wish it were possible for me to tell you now of the many, many things Father has said about you since you left. I know of no one in the world he loved more dearly than you. Of course you do not need anyone to tell you that. We have all been greatly blessed by his life of usefulness, his devotion to purpose, his integrity in business dealings, and his complete unselfishness and generosity.

With much love from all of us here, I remain

Devotedly,
Sam

Robert E. Harwell to Colie

Nashville
Thursday, April 27, 1944

Dear Colie—

Father has passed on, but I believe we will all feel his presence even more than ever before.

My last recollection of him was the day after his birthday when he was here at the store—he and Uncle Judge and Uncle Riggs sitting together in Sam's office, and his delight in having them with him. I walked with him as he went down the aisle of the store, and I stood at the door as he and Uncle Judge and Uncle Riggs went across the walk and got in his beautiful car and drove away. Compared to Uncle Judge, he did not appear active, but he was happy and on his way home. That was the last time I saw him before he died.

Never since you have been away have I missed you so much as I did Friday and Saturday. You can rest assured, however, that all of us believe that everything went just as Father would have it: no great mourning, but only an amazing consciousness of his presence, and the fact that he will live in our memories always.

Devotedly,
Rob

Ann to Colie

Nashville
Friday, April 28, 1944

Darling—

We are all going on here as normally as possible. I have refused everything for this week because I felt that is what you would want me to do—have also talked Clurie out of a big birthday party—

Sam K. Harwell Sr., W. E. "Judge" Harwell, and H. Riggs Harwell.

promising her we will do it in the summer. Marie and Mort are still in Grandpa's house but will gradually move over to their place. The house was left to Sam—John Barksdale is sending you a copy of the will—which I thought was very fair.

This is a glorious day—as soon as I get this posted I am going to go out and thin the broccoli plants which are already up in the cold frame. Then at noon I go to Thayer Hospital for my afternoon at the desk. I always enjoy it—and find that the change and contacts there do me a world of good. It makes me feel closer to all you are doing and seeing to be in touch with the military.

The girls are fine—I wish you could see Carolyn's hair now—it is growing very fast and is beautiful and so curly I can hardly comb it out properly. Clurie is in fine fettle these days—she has been outdoors a great deal and seems happier and brighter than usual. She and her friends spend much time digging foxholes in the orchard. Mother objects, but I say let them alone—it really doesn't matter and they have a wonderful time.

Devotedly,
Ann

Ann to Colie

Nashville
Sunday, April 30, 1944

Darling—

I have finally gotten around to doing something about a trip for myself. Briggs is still in New York. I can't get anyone to go with me, so am planning to leave by myself Tuesday morning. It all sounds absurd—but I'm tired of doing the sensible thing—I'm about ready to do something a little bit silly—and goodness knows, I need the change. I think a few days without any responsibility will be a godsend. If all goes well your next letter from me will be written in New York.

Devotedly,
Ann

CHAPTER EIGHTEEN

Small Realities

Colie to Ann

Italy
Tuesday, May 2, 1944

My dearest—

After a day of almost continuous activity, I set out for my favorite walk, which overlooks a peaceful, lovely scene, a rolling area of endless tiny gardens. Many of them were being worked—some of the men had their trousers rolled to their knees and were barefoot in the rich dirt. In one plot they were gathering onions. Others were gathering beautiful green leaf lettuce. The pink and white blossoms of the fruit trees are at their best and the trees are full-bodied. The stream was running swiftly in the deep valley beyond, the waterfall was pouring out of the opposite hillside—I thought to myself, I will say to Ann, this is where I used to walk in the afternoons, this is why I said it was so pretty, now do you see why? And I knew you would see why.

It is very hard to say to you what I want to say, even though I can feel your presence in this room. The things in my heart are not things you can read, they are things you have to speak in words that can't be chosen, nor long remembered. They are words that must be heard, that would not be meaningful to someone else. Just as when I begin a letter, I write, "My dearest." Did I ever call you that? I don't remember. I'm sure I don't know what I would say to you if you walked into this room now, but I know the words would be there and you would understand them. Just as you know how much I love you, how deep in my being there is a devotion to you, how vibrant that devotion is. Every hour of the day and night there is a thought for you, a word to be said, a glance to be exchanged, a hand that reaches out to be touched. Those are not the words, but I know they suggest them to you. And I could not pass this hour, this night, without feeling that I had said to you this something of love. The remembrances, the anticipation are my greatest strength—they alone bear me through the devastating flashes of loneliness. So I work, I laugh, I find joy in new friends, I come to a day's end with a feeling of satisfaction, I awaken to a new one with eagerness, I listen now to a violin *obbligato* on the radio and find it very beautiful. Not words—love is life itself.

Always devotedly,
Colie

Ann to Colie

New York City
Wednesday, May 3, 1944

Darling—

Here I am in New York and at the Ritz. When I checked in this morning and asked the price of the room—the clerk told me Mr. Evans had already taken care of that—it was extremely thoughtful of him.

I came up alone—but I have already talked to Sarah Ide and Dort and am planning to call others—so perhaps I will see more of my friends this way and really get more rest. New York seems a funny place to come for a rest! I really hated to leave my girls—when I couldn't get anyone to come with me—Clurie looked wistful and said, "Mummy, I'll go." It seems utterly pointless to be here without you. Lord, how I miss you!

Devotedly,
Ann

Colie to Carolyn

Italy
Thursday, May 4, 1944

My darling little girl—

This letter is written for your birthday. You are now a great big girl—five years old. I wish I could be there to help you celebrate.

It is fun to have a birthday party, for then you can have the people you like best come to see you—you can play games and dress in your nicest clothes and you can have ice cream and cake. I would certainly like a dish of ice cream. I believe I would like chocolate best, but strawberry would be mighty good, too. That is a strange thing about Italy, you don't see much ice cream. That is because they don't have as many cows to give milk as we have and because there are not so many electric freezing machines here. That is just one of the many reasons why Nashville and other cities in the United States are nice to live in. But there are many good things about Italy, too.

If you'd like to know what an Italian town looks like, just imagine there are a lot of little stone houses built all together on a hill in Percy Warner Park. Then you know what Italian towns are like. Someday I hope I can bring you and Lolly and Mummy to see this little town.

I know you are going to have a happy birthday. I am very proud of how big and smart you are. I know you are enjoying school and being a big help to Mummy and Grandmother. Give them and Lolly my love. I miss you and love you very much.

Your devoted,
Daddy

Colie to Marie Harwell Howell, Sam K. Harwell Jr., and Robert E. Harwell

Italy
Saturday, May 6, 1944

Dear Sister, Sam, and Rob—

This morning I heard of Father's death. The news came in a letter from a friend. There was merely this line, "I extend my deepest sympathy to you for the passing of your father this Friday A.M." First

I put the letter aside and thought that it was a mistake. Then I read the letter again and thought of the man who'd written it, and realized he did not make such mistakes, and knew that it was true. I want to tell you how I felt then and how I feel now. I thought: Father will not be there when I get back. He will not be sitting with my little girls at his knees as I have so often imagined him. He will not again extend his hand in that calm, gracious dignity that recognized, even between father and son, a mark of human importance that revealed his whole view of life. There will not be the constant source of good counsel, the calm judgment that refused to acknowledge the existence of an unwise course, that turned you from it as though it did not exist.

A world had seemed to be built around him, a very real world, of people who were good and no good, of people who varied somewhat and yet were constant in their pattern, of houses that were built right and wrong, of food and land and fences, of strength and weakness, of money and goods and people who paid for their goods and those who didn't, of children and grandchildren, of responsibilities. I thought: that was his world. I am thankful that I have known it and been a part of it and have shared it so fully.

I am sorry that I am not there to accept my part of the responsibilities. And I am thankful that all three of you and your families are there, grateful to Sam and Rob for again taking on my share of the responsibilities.

As for me, I am extremely busy and glad to be so. I wish I could write you in greater detail, but I can only say that I am fortunate to have such responsibilities and opportunities to see this job through. In Father's words, it couldn't be a more active job.

My love to you all, to your families and, as always, my lasting gratitude for sharing that love with mine.

Devotedly,
Colie

Colie to Ann

Italy

Saturday, May 6, 1944

My dearest—

I have just heard today of Father's death. I have written Sister, Sam, and Rob of my reactions, my first disbelief, my later realization that it was true. It was very difficult to face, but I cannot say whether it was more or less so because of the way the news came. It came at an extremely busy time for me, just when I was beginning meetings with officials of this town and the other towns which I administer. Perhaps it was fortunate for me this was true, as I went on and held the meetings and all day long was involved in seemingly endless problems that always are at hand. Then, this evening I tried to write a letter to them and it was very hard to write. Now I find it easier to write, easier to face this tremendous reality—I have thought many times today of you and your relationship with Father and of the children. I am grateful to you for having played such a fine role in his life, grateful that you and the girls have known him so lovingly, grateful for the friendship of your mother, grateful that you have understood my devotion to him and seen what he has meant to me. I remember you said that perhaps I would not see him again. It was very logical and you were right to urge me to see him as much as I could then.

Devotedly,

Colie

At the time he learned about his father's death, Colie was adjusting to his duties as CAO [Civil Affairs Officer] in the town of Isernia. He wrote in his personal journal about the needs there, such as "grain for the mill, farina for Isernia, farina for the stockpile, typhoid cases shipped to Campobasso."

He mentioned Italians such as "Cerosuola ready and smiling at every call, Renzi sharp and industrious, Lombardi a man you'd be wary of in a deal, but doing a proud job for his town;

the gracious little *podesta-sindaco* who gets things done; the Mother Superior, shrewd, capable, with strong hands and face."

He wrote of his British associates, like "the Group Captain and his quiet inspiration of men, a Montgomery type, [and] straight to the letter Giffin, a good officer to work for."

Finally, he noted the death of a boy, and "Flowers in the hands of [his] shattered mother [who was] wailing, 'Figlio, Figlio,' and the little fellow lies there in death's stillness."

"Did I wonder why I came here?" he concluded, "Who and what and why is AMG? It seems impossible now that anyone could have wondered."

Ann to Colie

New York City
Tuesday, May 9, 1944

Darling—

Have just come in from an evening with the Ides. We had dinner at the Persian Room at the Plaza and heard Hildegarde—she's really marvelous—I leave here Friday afternoon. I am eager to get started south but Sam asked me to do some buying for McClure's and I couldn't get the job finished by tomorrow—so have added two days on to the length of my stay.

Devotedly,
Ann

Colie to Ann [with copies to family members]

Italy
Tuesday, May 9, 1944

Dear family—

Today I received a number of letters which have been of great help. They have made it possible for me to talk in the light of the fuller knowledge of the time and manner of Father's death, even in the now complete realization that it was true, although there was no doubt at all in my mind. It would have been nearly impossible to talk freely about it had not these letters come today.

In one of her beautiful letters Ann expressed the thought that others have touched on and that has been in my mind, that somehow it has seemed fitting that I should be doing what I am at the time of his death, and with a job before me that could not be denied, one that required whatever skill and tact in dealing with people I might have been able to absorb in the rich years of Father's precept. As I talked with these people and considered their problems, urging, cajoling, discounting, trying to make the play and see it, too, I felt his strong character, assurance, and approbation. Not the least of his powers was that of approval.

I consider it remarkable that, although I am now thirty-eight, the youngest of the children, even I have known so many fine years of association and friendship with him and inspiring guidance. Now I am thankful for happy and inspiring memories so deeply ingrained in my life that they shall live as long as I do.

All the letters received today told beautifully and fittingly the last chapter of Father's great life story. But the last letter I opened was in a way best of all. It was from Father, written April 20, telling me of his birthday celebration, sending news of Ann and the girls as he always did, ending, "I will be mighty glad when we have won the war and have suitable peace again."

To all the family, each and every one, my devoted love and gratitude, my lasting thoughts.

Devotedly,
Colie

Sam K. Harwell Jr. to Colie

Nashville
Tuesday, May 16, 1944

Dear Colie—

Rob and I, in your absence, have qualified as executors of Father's estate. We have a complete feeling of agreement on all matters. I know of nothing that Father desired more than to have his children love, respect, admire, and help one another. That must and will be our entire purpose in carrying out the instructions of his will.

We are now considering the sale of his Cadillac car. He made no disposition of this in his will and we will sell it, we think, to a nice advantage. Father always believed in making a good trade. As his executors we have fifteen months to wind up the estate. Our advisors on all matters will be the three people in whom Father had the greatest degree of confidence. Hilary Osborn will be our advisor on matters pertaining to taxes. John Barksdale will be the authority on matters of a legal nature. Walton Garrett will handle details and keep complete records on every transaction.

As far as his home is concerned, there is the provision that I can purchase the home if I so desire, but if I do, the proceeds are to be divided equally between you, Sister, and Rob. I have not tried to think much about what we should do regarding this part of his will and will not make a hasty decision. We love our home. Josephine has spent lots of time and thought in fixing it up and it would not be easy to leave it. Sister and Morton, for the time being, will continue to live at Harding Place. Before any of the treasures there are in any way disposed of or divided, you will be taken into every detail and your wishes given every consideration. We will carefully carry on Father's farming activities just as though he were here and we will look after your interests as closely as though they were our own.

Neely, Harwell & Company will continue through this year on its present arrangement, as provided for in the contract. Before the end of this year we will make a new contract, in which you will be included. We will try to make the kind of contract Father would have wanted us to make. No man ever loved a business any more than he loved this one and when I say this one, I mean he loved the people here—all those of us who worked here. He was proud of our accomplishments. In every business move we make, we will have his vacant chair as a constant reminder of his counsel and advice and we will make no move without giving his advice, which we know by heart, our lasting consideration.

Your devoted brother,
Sam

Ann to Colie

Nashville
Thursday, May 18, 1944

Darling—

Your letter in which you spoke of hearing about Grandpa arrived yesterday. I know how you must feel—there is something about losing a parent that shakes the very ground under your feet—it is not only a personal loss but somehow the passing of an era. Mother and I had lunch with Marie day before yesterday—and it is strange—but when you go in the house you feel that Grandpa is still there—his personality still dominates the house and I have the feeling that his was such a strong spirit that it will go on forever.

All my love,
Ann

Ann to Colie

Nashville
Friday, May 19, 1944

Darling—

This afternoon at 5:30 we went to Parmer School to Leila's graduation from the eighth grade. There was as much going on as if they were graduating from college. All the little girls had on long dresses and the program was a long one with all the honor students having speeches. We went bearing gifts, of course—the most important of which was your doll from Italy.

I felt rather dreary without you in New York, but now that I have had the trip everyone says I look better. I think the change of scene did the trick. I've actually taken on a little weight since my return—something I have been trying to accomplish for some months now. The actual mechanics of traveling weren't bad until I got ready to leave—Pennsylvania Station was a madhouse—you could barely walk through the throngs of people—and I had to carry my bags for some distance before I was able to snag a redcap.

Devotedly,
Ann

Colie to Ann

Italy
Friday, May 19, 1944

My dearest—

I didn't get off a letter last night because when I came in from fishing I was too tired for anything but bed. Went over late in the afternoon and Borah and I spent about an hour and a half on the creek and walking up and down some of the steepest hills you've ever seen. The stream is beautiful, with marvelous rapids and many pools, shaded stretches and open ones. The scenery outdid the fish. I muffed two beautiful chances with trout, but at least had the thrill of "almost." While we ate at Borah's lodgings, his guide brought in two beauties (probably caught with worms) and I bought them—brought them home to prove my prowess. Alberto will do wonders with them for lunch.

Devoted love to all. My heart to you—

Colie

Ann to Colie

Tuesday, May 23, 1944

Darling—

This has been one of those days when I haven't been off the premises—have spent a good part of it working in the garden—trying to get the borders free of weeds. The ground is so dry it is like concrete—consequently I did a lot of hoeing and now I am so sleepy I can scarcely keep my eyes open. I called the Club today and arranged for the children to take swimming lessons—they start the first of June and I am going to let them take for only seven weeks because I'm hoping to get them away for a couple of weeks the end of July or the first of August.

We have heard no more from Briggs since I left New York. He doesn't know whether he will continue with the present organization or go in the Army.

What a life—and yet with all the heartaches and problems—I still find it satisfying. Particularly now, sitting here writing you with a divine breeze blowing through the window here in the library. I get an enormous amount of strength from this place—There are many things about the decorations that I am eager to change but by and large it is home and I love it. It will be so wonderful when you get back—then home will take on new meaning—the thought is so beautiful it overwhelms me.

Devotedly,

Ann

Ann to Colie

Saturday, May 27, 1944

Darling—

Carolyn sends the following message, "Dear Daddy: I miss you. I hope you are having a good time in the war. I am sorry for the men who get bombed. To Daddy in Italy from Carolyn."

Clurie has gone with the Willses to hear Dunninger—the man who reads your mind. I'm curious to see what she will get out of it.

The place looks wonderful—Mike is a miracle at making things look trim. This was the week to cut the grass—the borders are in better shape than they have ever been—and I'm busy now trying to get some annuals ready to go in them. Another week and they will be big enough to move—zinnias, marigolds, cosmos, verbena, petunias, sweet william, and scabiosa. As soon as they are large enough to take out of the frame I am going to start some perennial seed—so I will have some things that will continue to come up every year.

This is being written primarily as a birthday letter—thirty-nine—it doesn't seem possible. When I was in New York, Altman was advertising a rather ingenious arrangement—a series of eight packages, none of which could weigh over eight ounces—which is all we are allowed to send without a request. I ordered the set for you as a sort of progressive birthday present. I thought you might enjoy the fun of opening them and wondering what the next would be.

Last night I suddenly thought—this couldn't be me. Colie hundreds of miles away—in the middle of a war while I go on here alone. Soon I will wake up and find the whole thing was only a figure of the imagination. What has our generation failed to do that our homes and lives should be so confused, so distorted? It's as though I were seeing my life projected on a screen. Surely, I'll wake up tomorrow to find you in the bed next to mine. The whole thing is unbelievable. And yet every ounce of my being knows that it is real— there's nothing quite so real as loneliness, as empty arms. But praise God, it must end sometime.

Devotedly,
Ann

Ann to Colie

Nashville
Monday, May 29, 1944

Darling—

You spoke of receiving your father's will—Clurie has already asked me how much Grandpa left and I had to honestly say I didn't know. Yes, it was a wonderful will—I agree with you. I haven't heard Sam say whether or not he is going to take the house. Marie and Mort are still there but are planning eventually to move back to their own place.

Buying for McClure's was fun but hard work—I had to get up and out of the hotel several mornings by 8:30, so my trip was not so much sleeping as it was getting a new slant on things. Sam seems pleased at what I got, though many things have not yet come in—the dresses which have already arrived have sold well—so well, in fact, they are nearly all gone. I should like to do it again—though it was as hard work as I have ever gotten into. I'm going to get my railroad fare paid for doing the job—which will help considerably.

All my love,
Ann

Colie to Ann

Monday, May 29, 1944

My dearest—

This afternoon, I repaired with George Brooke and another officer to our neighboring sulphur baths. It is a former resort, located on a hillside of olive groves and rose gardens, overlooking a lovely valley with little towns perched on the distant hills. The baths are not too chic at present, but there are tubs, the water was steaming hot, and what more could you ask. We took the sun for a half hour, then into the steaming tub. It was definitely, as George would say, a proper bath. I came out infant pinkish and unknown to myself in the mirror; strangely also, instead of having that usual after-bath chill, I was warm. And so completely relaxed that I wouldn't need to fall asleep to be unconscious.

Now I have come in from the office, have heard the news with George, poured myself a small drink of restorative, have opened the windows across the table from me so that the waning sun can pour in, plus the sounds of some lads playing football, an occasional bird's song, a rooster proclaiming he is the big cheese in all this land. I can see the fields and hills beyond, green with trees and new grain, a pink stuccoed farm community outlined against early evening patches of sunlight and shade. All of that, I believe, describes how I feel. I am so very much at peace with all this world, I am sure that proves the point, for it would be quite easy to be and think and see and feel otherwise.

Give Clurie and Carolyn a good hug for me. Here are a few thousand for you.

Devotedly,
Colie

CHAPTER NINETEEN

Another Summer Begins

Anne Williamson McLemore to Colie

Nashville

Thursday, June 1, 1944

Dearest Colie—

Ann's trip to New York did much for her, she came home with new interest in the routine of home, and with a sparkle in her eyes and elasticity in her step—She really has measured up wonderfully— never a complaint and naturally her little shoulders have more burdens—but she goes with her head up and the confidence of a thoroughbred. But enough about my child, more about yours. The girls are growing stronger and more adorable, fast taking on manner- isms of older girls—Clurie reading everything and quite responsive with people—Carolyn eager to be just as old and to be able to read— Carolyn's hair is the most beautiful I have seen and the curls in the sunlight like burnished gold—

The cherry trees in the orchard were filled to the top branch and to get ahead of the birds, I got on a ladder and gathered enough to can twelve pints—The only thing lacking is slacks and I think "Grandmother" is going to indulge, if war continues and labor gets more scarce—

Our roses have been beautiful—during May, we would gather from thirty-five to fifty a day—The house was perfumed like a garden, and we gave many away—I put out twelve very fine bushes, so each day the lovely buds, just ready to unfold, are put between your two pictures on the living room table—

I know each member of the family has written in detail of your father's passing—Such a sweet good night for a busy, successful man.

This year, he had seemed to grow mellow and very tolerant—He and I had formed a sweet and understanding friendship, as the two grandparents—

Many afternoons he would send for me to come and sit with him, or have dinner when Marie and Morton would be away—and I do feel that I was able to help him through some lonely hours—always he would talk a great deal of you, what friends you were, and I think you satisfied every ambition he had for you—

The little girls seemed to grow quite into his life and his arms— I think they miss him keenly, and always speak of going to "Grandpa's house"—I am glad they are old enough to have known the sweet memories and to love that home—

We do miss you, and we speak of you many times during the day—You are so much in our hearts, that we can't realize you are so far away—May God keep you safe, for you are very precious to me—

Devotedly,
Mother Mac

Marie Harwell Howell to Colie

Nashville
Thursday, June 1, 1944

Dearest Colie—

The above date seems a fitting one to send birthday greetings with love and all good wishes, and may the day of victory and peace be hastened. The news I have heard just this minute sounds hopeful—as the Allies come nearer the eternal city. Our news here is that Mortie and Nancy were with us from Wednesday last through Sunday and we had the sweetest time together. A letter from Mortie tells us of his promotion to First Lieutenant—Sam has telephoned twice, and sent a picture in full flying outfit, standing by his trainer plane number 54—and looking pleased and happy—

Ann had such a lovely gathering the other afternoon preceding our invitation to Rolling River in honor of Mortie and Nancy. Practically none of Mortie's friends were here, so she had her friends just as Rob and Jane did—we had all the family for them on Wednesday, the first night they were here—the only outsiders being the Warfield family—They in return had us to a lovely breakfast on Sunday morning—

Your letters have been wonderful. I could picture you the day the news came to you—It was terrible to hear in such a way, the thing we thought to avoid by sending it through the Red Cross—Papa always said in speaking of you, "Coleman is where he should be," "He would be very unhappy not to be doing his part at a time like this," "He had to get in," and so on, they were the words he would use when he spoke of you. Mort and I are going on here in the big house for the time being, Mackey is so good and faithful, he was truly devoted to Papa—

Love and Happy Birthday,
Sister

Robert E. Harwell to Colie

Nashville
Thursday, June 1, 1944

Dear Colie—

All of us miss Father very much, but I am surprised how close I feel his presence. It's almost as if he is coming to the store every day. So many of his old friends and customers come in telling us of remarks which he made to them and valuable advice which he gave. Often these people say that his influence and direction counted greatly in their success. Apparently, he always had the right thing to say to people.

We have done nothing toward disposing of any of Father's things as yet. We have agreed to let John Barksdale buy his Belle Meade Club membership, which will bring $500–$600. We are also trying to dispose of his car, and it appears now that $2,500 will be a good price for it. He has cattle that should be sold in June, and he also has his farms in Giles and Marshall counties, which we are preparing to dispose of in some way. As to his stocks, they will probably be equally divided among us. His interest here in Neely, Harwell & Co. and our partnership contract must remain for the duration of this partnership.

I trust that you will spend a happy birthday this year and that things continue to go well with you. We think only of having you home, but when we read your letters, we realize that when you do come home, you will have something that will mean so very much to you and to all of us. We are proud of you and what you are doing. I am sure nothing in Father's last year brought more satisfaction than the fact that you were doing your part in the biggest job in history.

Devotedly,
Rob

On June 5, the U.S. Fifth Army entered Rome, making it the first Axis European capital to fall to the Allies.

Ann to Colie

Nashville
Monday, June 5, 1944

Darling—

I am so excited about the news of Rome—it came out yesterday and is too good to be true. I'm wondering now what kind of shape the place is in after the Germans have been there so long.

More tonight—I love you very much—

Ann

On June 6, D-Day, "Operation Overlord," began as Allied troops landed on the northern coast of France.

Ann to Colie

Nashville
Tuesday, June 6, 1944

Darling—

I'm almost afraid to get away from the radio—but I did want you to have some word from me on this momentous day. The invasion news is staggering—Last night at about 3:00 the air raid sirens blew—the first I knew of it was when Clurie woke me up asking what all the noise was. In my sleepy stupor I failed to realize what was going on—but many people got up and turned on their radios. I could kick myself for being so sleepy. Consequently the first I knew of it was this morning when the paper was brought in—then I realized what all the noise was last night.

The whole country is completely overcome—there have been many prayer services—Mother went to the one at War Memorial this morning—and the story is that one minister here went down at 4 A.M. and opened his church. President Roosevelt goes on the air at 9:00 tonight with a prayer. The radios have cut through programs all day with bits of news.

The *Tennessean* came out with the first story—and were intensely pleased with themselves. I talked to Mac this morning and he said you would certainly have enjoyed it. I felt like saying you were a heck of a lot closer to it than he is—The more I think about it the more astounded I become—to think how it was possible to coordinate such an enormous mass of men, planes, and ships—the news indicates that there were 11,000 planes and over 4,000 ships used in the operation.

Take care of yourself, darling—you mean everything to me. My constant prayer is that God will see fit to bring you back to me.

Devotedly,
Ann

Colie to Ann

Italy
Tuesday, June 6, 1944

My dearest—

I am in my elegant office at the *Municipio* trying to beat the last fading moments of daylight but realizing I probably will have to finish with a candle. The marshal of *carabiniere* has come in to report on some problems, then some others. Afterwards my aide, Lieut. the Earl of Shrewsbury, came in and we chatted about our problems of the day and morrow.

At the moment, I am very fortunate in that I am in a beautiful little city and apparently things are going along well. There is a great deal of interest here, churches, fine buildings, beautiful homes, attractive people, several of whom speak English. Most interesting of all was to find that a group of liberal, Allied sympathizers had taken over the government and put such big shots, as had not fled already, into jail. I believe we now have officials on the job and on the way back to normalcy.

Love,
Colie

Colie's calendar notes that he was in Subiaco on June 9.

Colie to Ann

Italy
Friday, June 9, 1944

My dearest—

I am in a very nice six-room apartment and have a cook (Mateelda) and her husband (Giovanni) looking after things. John Shrewsbury, an extremely likeable young fellow, and Maj. Frisker, a visiting specialist, have rooms with a marquise, but eat with me. The place is adequately furnished. Its main charms are a perfectly equipped bathroom with flushing toilet (a change), a complete kitchen, a big bedroom looking out over a spectacular valley. I have a little desk before a window and the sun is pouring in. I've just had a cup of tea and John tells me breakfast is ready. This is the prettiest town I've seen with lovely houses and beautiful churches. Yesterday I let them hold a big church festa, "Corpus Domine," concluding with a speech by the Bishop before the piazza church. We stood on our office balcony and it was a beautiful ceremony.

Colie

Ann to Colie

Nashville

Saturday, June 10, 1944

Darling—

This in quotes is from Carolyn—"Mummy took a picture of us when I was holding my dolly and Lolly was standing up straight and I was five and she was eight. And our shadows were showing behind us. And I took swimming lessons and can stay under the water. I can swim on my back and on my tummy with somebody holding me. We hope we are coming up to see you if you are there where you are after the war is over. And I wish you were here because I want you to watch me take my swimming lesson. My dolly watches me. Happy birthday, dear Daddy—happy birthday to you. I hope you had a nice birthday and I hope you get pink and white ice cream."

I am still hungrily devouring all possible news of the European situation and have saved the papers put out the first two days. Would you consider keeping a sort of diary? We might do the same thing here—then after it is all over, we might combine the two. It occurs to me that the two points of view published together might be extremely interesting. What do you think?

Devotedly,

Ann

In a later report, Colie said that he and "Lt. the Earl of Shrewsbury arrived in Arsoli Saturday, 10 June, and took over administration of eleven communes: Arsoli, Anticoli,

Camerata Nuovo, Cineto Romano, Riofreddo, Roviano, Vallinfreddo, Vivaro Romano, Agosto, Cervara di Romana, Marana Equo."

Colie to Ann

Italy
Saturday, June 10, 1944

My dearest—

John (Shrewsbury), our driver, Private Leahy, and I have had an eventful day, plenty of work and customary laughter. The latter was occasioned with the fact that we are now occupants of an apartment in a gorgeous castle, replete with oil paintings, coats of mail, dark shadowy passages, moats and secret doors, not to mention balconies that overlook formal Italian gardens, the church piazza beneath, and ravines that drop hundreds of feet. Quite a contrast to our last stopping place where John and I threw all our stuff into one room in a bare, smelly building, I broke two of our four bottles of wine on the floor, the fresh cherries Leahy had nursed so lovingly scattered all over the floor, and it was a general mess. Now we have two beautiful bedrooms with modern furniture, a complete bathroom down to a wood burning water heater that provided me with an elegant bath, a kitchen replete with cook and maid, a large former bedroom in which we were served dinner in style from heavy tablecloth and napkins, and two larger rooms to use for offices. Also the Princess has advised us through the estate manager that we can use the state banquet hall for major conferences when we desire. It was with some chagrin that I advised her we would hardly need these latter facilities. The Princess, by the way, is no matter for concern, being a lady of large functions and proportions to match.

All this comes under the heading of the lighter side, but it has its importance from the serious view, too, since it is our responsibility to look after such estates and people. Speaking of people, we have met many fine ones. An incident you will enjoy was that I spoke in one place to bring news of what was going on in the world and also establish our identity there. A few words, but I am told they were rather

Coleman Harwell and Patrick Leahy, his driver.

well chosen, seemed to go over well with the populace, and the Bishop went so far as to compliment me thereupon.

A touch of civilization is right handy even in small doses. John and I are enjoying one another's company, which he remarked upon tonight. Another officer advised me that he was the premier earl of England, a fact you could readily believe he lives up to although there is not the slightest trace of upstage attitude about him. Tonight as we laid out our things for a luxurious stopover in our castle, he brought out his family pictures and then I brought out mine. One was of him and his very beautiful wife (next to mine the prettiest I've seen in many a moon) made in front of their house which is what you might expect of a 10,000 acre estate.

Devotedly,
Colie

Ann to Colie

Nashville
Sunday, June 11, 1944

Darling—

It gives me a terrific shock to realize that this time last year I was with you in Charlottesville. There have been so many heartaches in between, so many adjustments to be made. Someone said the other night—"I don't know how you women manage to look so well." I could have told them but didn't. We wear our widow's mantle proudly and sometimes even gaily—because we must at all costs hide the terrible loneliness in our hearts. And you are always so close to me in spirit—that realization gives me the strength to go on.

The other night Grace Gardner said she and Ed were going to Sea Island in August, and suggested we go along with them. This morning she said she was going to call the hotel there and did I still want to go? I said by all means, but that I didn't want them to feel in any way obligated to worry with us—she said Ed was delighted at the idea. In a few minutes she called me back and said she had our reservations—the girls and I will have one large room—we will go down around the early part of August. I'm really delighted—because I had to take the girls somewhere and it will be nice to have another couple around. We will only be gone two weeks from the time we leave until our return, which is about as much money as I want to spend. This way we will get back about a week before school starts—and Clurie will be fresh for the fall.

Devotedly,
Ann

Colie to Ann

Italy
Monday, June 12, 1944

My dearest—

John and I have a suite in the castle furnished with modern things; there is a boxspring bed that is the first I have seen in many a day and the heavy linen sheets are something I had long since forgotten. The maid brought up a delightful tray of coffee (with the best elements of American and Italian brew combined), crisp bacon, and bread and jam, and a plate of luscious black cherries. Now I am sitting before a window that overlooks the formal garden in which the fountain plays continuously. We have a large bathroom and downstairs there are three other rooms at our disposal in addition to the kitchen. The administrator of the estate provided the cook and maid and offers all other hospitality of the place. The Princess was very gracious upon our arrival, showing us her apartment. We have not seen her since, but I think we will ask her to tea with us in the garden terrace and thereby express our appreciation for her hospitality.

Tell Clurie and Carolyn I'll look forward to telling them how it feels to visit in a real castle of a real princess.

All my love,
Colie

Sam K. Harwell Jr. to Colie

Nashville
Tuesday, June 13, 1944

Dear Colie—

We are all thinking of you today on your thirty-ninth birthday and hoping you are well and happy.

Your expression of appreciation for the few little things that I have been able to do for you has done something to me. I feel unworthy of such an expression. Every thing I have been privileged to do has brought me great pleasure. So few opportunities come for me to show my willingness to be of some assistance. I remember the expression "He also serves who stands and waits." I stand and wait at your command and also at the command of your family. I hope they know how anxious I am to be of any service possible.

I don't have to tell you how much we miss Father. His chair in my office is still in place and many times during the day I have a feeling that he is there, ready to advise or comfort as the case may be. I find myself continually thinking of what Father would say about this or that in connection with the problems of business, farming, home life, social activities, church affairs and many other matters too numerous to mention.

I am glad to report all is well at home. We went to church Sunday with Ann and after church we picked up the children at Sunday School and enjoyed their company for the trip home. This included a brief stop at Weise's Pharmacy, where Ann bought ice cream for the noonday luncheon which, of course, pleased Carolyn and Ann McClure very much. The girls are looking fine and Ann seems very happy—looks fine and is most enthusiastic over the many wonderful letters which we continue to get from you.

With much love from all of us here at home, I remain,

Devotedly your brother,

Sam

Ann to Colie

Tuesday, June 13, 1944

Darling—

I couldn't let the day go by without sending you a word on your birthday. I hope you received the cable and letter—also the package I have sent from Altman's. I have thought of you all day and wish that it might be a happy one for you.

All my love, darling,

Ann

Ann to Colie

Wednesday, June 14, 1944

Darling—

I am having some portraits done of the children—by a man who does pastels for $45 each—his work is good—and I have been eager for some portraits of the children before they get any older—Carolyn's hair is beautiful and Clurie lovely with her summer coat of tan—and they change so rapidly. I wanted to catch them while they are at their best.

I love you,

Ann

Colie to Ann

Italy

Thursday, June 15, 1944

My dearest—

In a moment I will mount my horse cart and head for one of my communes. Lack of passable roads makes this necessary, not to mention absence of gasoline. Have discovered one of my places is an artists' colony, one of the most beautiful locations you've ever seen, and a delightful old Britisher who came out to meet me just as though he'd stepped out of Mr. Chips—

Devotedly,
Colie

Ann to Colie

Friday, June 16, 1944

Darling—

This has been a busy day. Carolyn sat from 11:00 until 4:30 having her picture done—She was amazing about it—and more patient than I would have been—the child has just plain "guts." The picture is very good—he has gotten her exactly—she has on a yellow dress and a yellow bow in her hair. He does Ann Sunday and I'm eager to see if he can catch the beauty in her face. She weighs 65 pounds—is getting very brown from swimming and looks more robust than I remember. Tomorrow afternoon she is having Martha Casey, Ellen, and Florence Fletcher to play and I have permitted them ice cream and cake.

All my love,
Ann

Colie to Ann

Italy
Saturday, June 17, 1944

My dearest—

What beautiful country we've seen. John just remarked that his best impression of the day was of the great, gorgeous fields of grain being harvested by hand. When you're living rather close to the market basket and every fellow is counting his rations closely, you appreciate those things tremendously. In many places children stand on the road and throw flowers as we pass. They have reminded me so much of Clurie and Carolyn. How I love you and miss you and wish you could see this gorgeous country with me now.

Devotedly,
Colie

By June 17, Colie was in Todi.

Colie to Ann

Italy
Saturday, June 17, 1994

My dearest—

This is written from a hotel room in a beautiful little Italian town, the kind you have to see to believe. We delight in the presence of electricity, which I had almost forgotten existed—the castle is no more for me, but I am pleased to have John Shrewsbury's company again. We enjoy working as a team and he is one of the most pleasant young men I have known. Yesterday some peasants stopped us along the road with baskets of peaches and I bought two kilos for forty lire. Several times I have been greeted with quantities of luscious cherries, the rich black type. I had a great experience in one of the lovely little towns a while back where I resolved the differences of the two factions by appointing a Jewish *sindaco*, a man who had been hiding in the caves. He was a

Todi.

delightful gentleman and the priests, politicos, and peasants all regarded him as the outstanding man of the town. As we drove away (in my borrowed horse cart) a mother told her child to start clapping and all the townsfolk joined in. Then the *contadini* driving me turned and said, "Everybody likes the governatore," which was about the nicest thing I've heard said in many a day.

Devotedly,
Colie

Ann to Colie

Nashville
Thursday, June 29, 1944

Darling—

I feel that life has so much to offer the two of us together—as though we might see one another with not only the same joy but with an added understanding, with something even more precious. It is as though this separation were a preparation for that fuller happiness that I know will be mine when we are together again. There are so many things I want us to do together—I want above everything else for you to find more time for the things that seem so real to me and I feel sure will to you too. Let's have less of the material things and more of the things of the heart and spirit—more time at home, as we did in Charlottesville—more time to see our children together—more time for our friends—more time to round this life out together.

I love you so much, darling,
Ann

CHAPTER TWENTY

All Goes Well

Colie to Ann

Italy
sometime in July 1944

My dearest—

I have the feeling of having made the wisest decision of my career in choosing this life and experience, and I cannot believe that anyone anywhere is having half the experience in scenery and personalities that I am having.

It is necessary sometimes to brace yourself and realize that in the course of the day you are living things you never dreamed of. Like signing a few sheets of paper and sending former Fascist bigshots back to a place where they will be less trouble. Or calling a troublesome one before you and telling him he goes in for a lockup and trial, and he says he has never done anyone harm and has always worked hard, and you tell him he will have ample opportunity to tell that to the court when he is tried, and he thanks you for that—And my wonderful interpreter who was a valet and private secretary for ambassadors and generals and titled personages, who takes my troublesome ways all day until 7:30 P.M. and is perfect in his humor and disposition—And my new mayor who pleaded not to be appointed since he had to make a living for his family, and he is doing such a sincere job for his town—and calling on the Bishop in his palace and he says I am gentile and simpatico both, quite the tops in compliments—then meeting him in the middle of the piazza and I tell him I am not a Catholic but much interested because I get much inspiration from Catholic services, and he says, "It is no difference, we are all children of God."

Devotedly,
Colie

Ann to Colie

Nashville
Saturday, July 1, 1944

Darling—

Briggs called from New York today—he is delighted with the way things have worked out—will be here for a month—then goes to Asia. Everything is straight with the draft board. We are all excited about having him. I think it will do the girls good to have a man around for a change and, of course, Mother is beside herself with joy.

I told Dibbie today at lunch that I was about ready to play a game of golf. Though with the girls' swimming lessons three mornings a week, I am pretty well tied up in the mornings. Then of course I go to the hospital on Friday. I am working in the wards now and finding it much more interesting than any other work I have done there. We see and talk to all kinds—they take us completely for granted which makes the work much easier and they are always courteous—there are always some who don't want to be bothered but most are glad to have someone to talk to. We are not allowed to sit on their beds and I spend the time leaning first to one side and then to the other talking my head off but mostly listening. I like it for many reasons—but mainly because it makes me feel closer to you.

All my love, darling—
Ann

Colie to Ann

Italy
Saturday, July 1, 1944

My dearest—

Sometimes my best war news comes from the *Tennessean*. At the moment we are well caught up with the news and have received some fairly recent army papers, but there have been times when we were isolated and when an army vehicle appeared, we would halt it on the road and ask what news they had—we arrived in one little town the day after the invasion of Europe. Of course we had no electricity and the town had no news.

I set off in a borrowed Jeep and several miles away located a unit that had a radio working. One of their officers had jotted down the news, so I was able to take it back and made a speech in the main piazza. Afterwards John said I was becoming quite adept at speech-making—I can imagine what great thrills there were when the news broke of the European front. It has been, you may be sure, of equal interest here. It has given new buoyancy to us in Italy to feel that Jerry [the German army] is being hit at another spot. The campaign here has been tremendous and I am grateful for having a small role in it. From the first gun of the great offensive, which I heard and saw with complete awe, it has been vast and brilliant—

One of the most gratifying things of this job has been the opportunity to serve with many units and commanders. My friends, many of whom I know by name and address, some of whom I know only by having shared common experiences, literally cover the world. Today I saw the smiling face of Staff Sergeant Kelly, who is the NCO boss of a hospital unit, and it was pleasant to know his outfit, where I have many friends, is nearby.

The responsibility is heavy, but the satisfaction is immense. In some towns there is a CAO, along with a town major, a labor officer, and many other specialists. Here you are all of it. You supply labor for the army, hold court on amazingly complicated and sensitive matters, straighten out (you hope) some of the most complex public benefit and finance matters you've ever heard of, try to get a food system back in order, direct an agriculture committee on plans for harvesting and threshing grain, select new officials, throw out old ones, track down fascists and brigands, set prices and try to combat the possibility of a black market, arrive at the office to find a fleet of trucks waiting to be loaded with grain, start leaving at 7:00 in the evening but have to sit a half hour while you explain to a woman why you sentenced her husband to jail for perjury.

Half a minute from us is the main promenade of the town, overlooking the vast green valley, where grapevines and fruit trees are in full leaf, where the grain is shocked in those individual patterns that no one can create but the Italians. The little park on the edge of the town was packed with families and courting couples, on the other side of the road there is a playground where two and three year olds, with hair trimly tied back in ribbons, were swinging and singing. There were blondes and redheads, sport outfits and blue and green and red dresses, and you felt that this was New York or Nashville and expected someone to speak English any minute.

My Italian is not much, but I understand enough to begin to feel at home with it, so I begin to find these people quite real—My window looks down upon a hillside of tile roofs and stucco houses that shine in the late evening sun. Across the rooftops is the beautiful Cathedral.

The other night we went to the home of the fiancé of one of our interpreters. I took one of your Altman packages that had just come, the box containing sugar-coated almonds. The fiancé's younger sister is named Anna and looks like a pretty blonde movie actress. I told her that your name was the same as hers and that our older daughter had the same name. They wanted to know all about you and the girls, and how old they were. Then the mother got out her collection of hand-painted Christmas cards, which seemed to be quite a treasury, and a set of cards of Italian native costumes and she gave me a whole set for you, as a compliment in return for the candy. The father, who was not there that night, is the Italian representative of Martini and Rossi vermouth, so they had some lovely liqueurs—There was also a young cousin, studious type with glasses, who reminded me of many an

American boy—We all sat around the table and had a nice evening. Such gatherings mean a great deal—

Your devoted,
Colie

Colie to Ann

Italy
Friday, July 7, 1944

My dearest—

Tonight I had the pleasant experience of a visit from the Bishop of our city. The Italians have a special way of doing things, abiding strictly by their version of the niceties, and I think none of them is more strict than churchmen. He had sent word several days ago that he wished to call one evening, so I sent word that this evening would suit me. He came at 9:30, a strangely local calling hour. We talked about many things, he told of his experiences in the church, and it was interesting to learn that several people I have met in my travels in Italy were friends of his, including the Bishop of another town (the one where I made the talk on invasion news). When he left, it was after curfew, so I walked home with him to the border of his estate.

Always,
Colie

Ann to Colie

Nashville
Saturday, July 8, 1944

Darling—

I decided to have Carolyn and Clurie's rooms repainted because they had gotten in such terrible shape with torn wallpaper that I was actually ashamed for anyone to go in them. The painters got out at noon today and we have been busy getting things back in shape. I had also taken down the curtains in our room and they had to go back. Then the hall doors which had not been painted looked terrible against the fresh new paint so I washed them as well as all the furniture in Clurie's room. The rooms look nice and you would be pleased.

Carolyn's is a lovely Williamsburg blue and Clurie's is grey with one wall done in red and gray paper. They are both delighted with them.

Devotedly,

Ann

Ann to Colie

Nashville

Sunday, July 9, 1944

Darling—

I am very much interested in hearing the patients at the hospital talk about the country you are in. Their stories are not nearly so glamorous as the ones you write to me. I wonder often if it isn't because you are merely giving me the glowing side of the picture.

This afternoon I took the girls to the pool for a swim. Clurie has been asking me if I could go off the diving board—so today I took courage in hand and dove off. I had to keep face—and it was fun. Clurie had gone home from church with the Sam Harwells for dinner—so we took Buddy with us too. Carolyn no longer jumps in feet first—she throws herself in the water—a sort of dive—but it invariably ends up a complete belly buster. She does very well. I'm delighted with her progress—and she has no more fear of the water than a fish.

Devotedly,

Ann

Colie to Ann

Italy

Tuesday, July 11, 1944

My dearest—

Yesterday I had lunch with Al Austin, John Clarke, and Main Albright. A regular homecoming. It is sad to think that Ken is now holding down the fort of our old homestead alone (with Assunta). Among other things, I had hoped the day would produce an opportunity to buy some American cigarettes, but I found there was no place to buy any, and John's own private PX did the job. He came through with a carton of Camels and four bars of soap. You would have loved seeing his private room in a swanky hotel, in which the largest item was a huge cask. I suggested it was wine, but he quickly pointed out that it was olive oil. I'll not be surprised to find a Shetland pony yet.

Your devoted,
Colie

Colie to Ann

Italy
Wednesday, July 12, 1944

My dearest—

This afternoon I visited two of my little communes, the last on foot as my borrowed Fiat couldn't ford the bridgeless river, went over country lanes, via an ancient ferry at one point, through such lovely back country as you'd never see without a driver who knows every inch of it—two delightful Italian officers for dinner. One produced a Rotary card he'd carried all through the war (forbidden as it is) with much pride.

Your always devoted,
Colie

Ann to Colie

Nashville
Wednesday, July 12, 1944

Darling—

We haven't had a real rain since the middle of May. Our soil soaker has completely given out on us—I got out with my needle and thread and tried to mend it this morning but found it to be a thankless job, so I called Eason-Morgan [the Eason-Morgan Co. sold paints, wallpaper, glass, and seed] and bought the last one in the store. I shall get busy on the tomatoes as soon as it arrives tomorrow. In two more weeks we are going to have worlds of tomatoes and I shall get busy and can some—I have just finished putting up ten glasses of jelly made from apples out of our own orchard and should be able to get enough later on to make two dozen glasses in all. Then in another two weeks the grapes should be ready and we'll make some of that. Food here continues to be very high—though I suppose compared to what you see there it would seem cheap.

Devotedly,
Ann

Ann to Colie

Nashville
Saturday, July 15, 1944

Darling—

This house is like the quiet after the storm. Briggs came in Thursday afternoon and last night we had all the Columbia and Alabama relatives for dinner—George, Mattie, Rebecca, Eleanor, Nonie, Bobby, Nellie, and Mary Major—as well as Billy Major and his wife. Jane and Rob had given me one of their nice legs of lamb—but yesterday morning I got worried and had fried chicken instead. It was a good thing I did because they really ate. I had to be at Thayer most of the day—so it was pretty hectic for me—especially the bartending—mixing for twelve people is no cinch. So when I finally got in bed at 11:30 I was so sleepy I could hardly read the paper. They were all very much interested in hearing about you and I even read them two of your letters. I much prefer your writing to that of John Hersey, and he is plenty good. Clurie was so wistful in talking about visiting in Columbia that they took her back with them. We've been having a lot of fun lately thinking how grand it would be if one of us were Superman—then the rest of us could hang on and fly over to see you.

We had a family dinner at Harding Place Thursday night and they were all very sweet and seemed interested in hearing what Briggs had to say. The children were busy doing all sorts of stunts like trying to stand on their heads—so Josephine and I went way in the back of the yard and did some handsprings for them—they thought that was wonderful.

Devotedly,
Ann

Ann to Colie

Nashville

Monday, July 17, 1944

Darling—

We are enjoying Briggs tremendously. Saturday night we went to the Nielsens and last night to the McNeills—tonight we are staying at home.

The Democratic convention opened in Chicago today. It seems unfortunate to me that the Democrats were unable to find anybody else—or perhaps Mr. Roosevelt would have run anyway—but it [his term of service] is just too long, Colie—and I can't get steamed up over Mr. Dewey. I would have felt differently about Bricker.

I miss you so much, darling—

Ann

On July 18, Colie left Todi and arrived in Umbertide.

Colie to Ann

Italy

Wednesday, July 19, 1944

My dearest—

I am the guest in a wonderful old fortress castle. The host is a charming young count who speaks perfect English (his mother was American). Also here is his lovely aunt, his cousins, Marquis and Marquise. We dined late and sat on the terrace until a moment ago. It was so cool that my field jacket was scarcely enough. The day was a pleasant one, almost without work, a rarity for me, and I went so far as to take a nap this afternoon—Many things continually amaze me, for instance the lack of ceremony and the great friendliness between masters of estates and their servants. At dinner, the servant carried on conversation in a pleasant, unobtrusive way; in the evening the servants gather about the family on the terrace, talk or sing or both—I brought out a pack of your instant coffee and one

Civitella Ranieri, "a wonderful old fortress castle."

of Sam's candy packages tonight, both warmly received.

Devotedly,
Colie

Ann to Colie

Nashville
Wednesday, July 19, 1944

Darling—

We are again in the midst of a bus strike—I had to take Briggs in to get the Columbia bus—he went down to get Clurie for me and they'll both be back today. Yesterday morning we went over to Harding Place and had one of Mackey's wonderful breakfasts— cantaloupe, scrambled eggs, fried tomatoes, bacon, coffee, and syrup.

The family are all scattering for the rest of the summer. Yesterday Jane, Robin, and Jonathan left for Vermont—where Louise Bray has a house—to be there the rest of the summer. Sunday, Sam, Josephine, and Sambo leave for a two week fishing trip to Canada. Sometime soon the Howells go to Beersheba—and we leave the eighth of August for Sea Island.

Devotedly,
Ann

Sam K. Harwell Jr. to Colie

Nashville
Thursday, July 20, 1944

Dear Colie—

This is one of those cool, lazy, rainy days that slip up on us in the middle of a hot spell in July here in Tennessee. It is a welcome change from the weather of the past few weeks, which has been extremely hot and dry. The clouds are low and the rain is falling gently. The Cumberland River is low and clear and it is pleasant to see the rain drops as they disturb the surface of this great old river. Those of us who have farm activities and gardens will welcome this shower.

Coleman Harwell II, Rob Harwell Jr., and Jonny Harwell.

All goes well on the home front, at least that part of it with which we are most vitally concerned. Your family are all well. We are looking forward to being with them this evening at Rolling River Farm, where Rob is acting as host for all members of the family who are here at the present time.

We will, no doubt, read several of your letters which Ann has just received and we will talk at length about you and the many interesting and varied experiences which are yours. We will also discuss at length the political situation at home and maybe listen to Mr. Roosevelt's speech of acceptance in his bid for a fourth term. We will talk about the progress of the war, the wonderful advances which we and our allies seem to be making on all fronts, and we will, no doubt, make some prediction as to when this mess will be over and the world can settle back into peaceful channels.

Miss Martha and Miss Ruth were delighted that you were getting the little packages. We are sending them out every few days and it does us all good that some of them come through. I am glad you are getting *Newsweek* and know you will find it interesting.

Wishing for your continued success in your work and praying for your continued well being, I remain,

Your devoted brother,
Sam

On July 20, the Democratic convention nominated Franklin D. Roosevelt for a fourth term as president.

Ann to Colie

Nashville
Saturday, July 22, 1944

Darling—

This is Carolyn's letter—"Dear Daddy—I miss you. And I want you to send me a Hershey bar if you can get it. And also Lolly misses you and Grandmother and Uncle Briggs and Mummy too. And also Lolly and Mummy and me are going to read a book this morning.

The name of the book is *The Magic Bed Knob*. We are going swimming tomorrow—Buddy was here last night spending the night.
And we played a game of Chinese checkers. We also will be glad
when the war is over—And Coleman is the cutest little boy of the
world that I know—and Coleman also has red hair like me and it is
curling up and one time we went out there and Uncle Sam said look
Colie look, and put something on his nose and he laughed. We rided
in the wagon and Sambo pulled us. I love you and also Mummy—I
love you so much. You are so sweet to help the people in the war. And
also we gave Blackout away."

Carolyn wants me to say something—it is, as always—that I love
you with all my heart—

Devotedly,
Ann

Colie to Ann

Italy
Sunday, July 23, 1944

My dearest—

In this castle you can wander about from room to room and fail
to find the least symmetry in any of it, but this should not be a point
of criticism, for the present owner is just taking over the place as heir
to his late uncle, and reassembling various items which had been
hidden from the Germans. It is a gorgeous setting and full of interest.
There are oddments of oil paintings and scrambled furniture, vaulted
ceilings, those strange sofas that fit into corners. My bedroom opens
on the outer courtyard, where the main gate stands and also there is
a statue of the founder somewhat battered by age and bad weather,
but still standing proudly.

The castle is located in one of the most beautiful of Italian valleys,
abundant with grapevines and trimmed trees that serve as forage for
the cattle and shade for crops that must stand the heat of late summer
when water is scarce. There is the winding river, the town below, lanes
through the woods, huge white oxen on the hillsides, most beautiful of

sunsets and the valley filled with clouds in the morning—And, oh yes, I have a bathroom in one of the turrets. Furthermore, it works. I had a hot bath yesterday morning—

Devotedly,
Colie

Ann to Colie

Nashville
Monday, July 24, 1944

Darling—

This time last year we were on our way to Charlottesville—I remember so vividly your standing out in front of the little house waving to us after we had driven too far up the street and had to turn and come back. And your taking us in and showing us the house with great pride—and our pleasure over it—that month was one of the precious spots in my memory—I shall never forget even the smallest part of it. I remember too the cool fresh mornings when I used to get in the car still half asleep and drive you over to the university, our memorable cocktail party as we passed the canapes and you were busily popping champagne corks, the nights when I used to sit on the sofa and pretend to read while you and Ed did German, the innumerable evenings when we seemed to feed half of the school—down to the time when you were alerted and the earth seemed to drop from under me— It is all a strange dream but strangest of all is this long year without you. I am grateful that your work means so much to you and that you have been able to find people who interest you so much—but I shall thank God when you can write finished to your job there and come home—back to the orchard in bloom in the spring—to the lighted fire in the evening—to the children gaily and hurriedly rushing off to school in the morning—Then once more my heart can skip a beat when I hear your car crunch the gravel in the driveway and I can again enjoy the luxury of picking up the phone and hearing your voice. Then the nights will no longer be just an endless sequence of hours—and the loneliness of an empty bed next to mine will be forgotten.

All my love, darling,
Ann

Colie to Ann

Italy
Monday, July 24, 1944

My dearest—

I have just come up to my room, with the assistance of my carbura lamp which Eugenio, the manservant of the house, lighted. It has been a delightful evening. We did not have dinner until 9:00, finished at 10:00, then went out for a breath of air. Everyone had gathered and Giorgio (the Marquis) brought out a gramophone. There were excellent records and several danced on the grass—principally Giorgio and his sister. My driver, also in the group, is a rather remarkable youngster who never likes anything or anybody when he arrives and winds up in love with everybody and with everybody crazy about him. They asked him to sing, which he did, and added to the pleasantness—an amazingly simple, homely, happy group. The old Marquise (Giorgio's mother) called time at midnight, so all is quiet in the castle walls now.

Devotedly,
Colie

Ann to Colie

Nashville
Sunday, July 30, 1944

Darling—

Last night I had my party for Briggs. It was wonderful but very tiring. When I finally got upstairs at 1:30 and took off my shoes I began to realize how tired I was—I don't think I had sat down once since the first guest arrived at 7:00. There were forty-six guests—and we had mint juleps first—I had scoured the town for mint and made a syrup—so there wouldn't be such a rush at the last minute—I had been saving up Bourbon—the juleps were a tremendous success—It was a very hot night so we had chairs all over the front lawn and it was lovely there. My little cook would find it impossible to handle such a gathering—so I had engaged Mrs. Eakin—who came in at 7:00 with the food, plates, silver, napkins, and waiters. The food was delicious and the whole thing went off like a dream. Darling, it would have pleased you so and you would have had such a good time because there would have been nothing to do but enjoy yourself and be attractive—which you do so superbly. I think I missed you more last night than I can remember.

Devotedly,
Ann

Ann to Colie

Nashville
Monday, July 31, 1944

Darling—

Many people here feel that the European part of the war will be over before too many months have passed—How do you feel about that? Do you feel that your place will continue to be in Italy or do you feel that you might end up in Germany? I am hoping the Russians will hurry and get in there. I think perhaps they might be a little tougher on the Germans than we—and from my point of view that would be excellent. We shouldn't forget too easily or we might have this whole job to do all over again.

Briggs and I went out to the Evanses' Sunday for a barbecue for the entire staff—The barbecue was delicious and there was beer— everyone was milling around playing ping-pong, croquet or something—and enjoying themselves. They all asked about you.

The Evanses had come to our party the night before and I brought out my one and only bottle of $6 Scotch for him. I was glad to do it since I could never have had the party in the first place without his Easter present.

The *Tennessean* has taken over a suite at the Hermitage Hotel— had it decorated—it is lovely—yesterday Mr. Evans had Briggs come down and have lunch with him—just the two of them. They ate

Anne McLemore, Clurie, Carolyn, Ann Harwell, and Briggs McLemore Jr.

in regal state in the dining room of the suite—had steaks and Mr. Evans had the chef come up to the room. Briggs loved it.

I love you,
Ann

CHAPTER TWENTY-ONE

The End of Summer

Colie to Ann

Italy
Tuesday, August 1, 1944

My dearest—

We are comfortably fixed in a house that has been well cleaned up and all we could ask would be water and light. But my lamp and our water cans do well enough for us. We could use windows to keep out the flies, but you come to be thankful that you've had all those inoculations and are supplied with mepacrine [anti-malarial] tablets and mosquito bars. Having been shy on the bathing side recently, I was pleased to find this afternoon that the drivers had rigged up a Goldbergerish affair with a hand pump leading into a tube and thence into a water sprinkler. So, I put on my swimming trunks and went into the backyard with soap and towel and had a thorough going over. I had just finished that when I recalled a bottle of cognac I had bought. So I got it out and poured a drink for those who cared to join and was just settled into a relaxed half hour before dinner when an officer arrived with the mail. All that has given me a wonderful evening indeed. (The mood seems to be general for the boys are making up a batch of tea in the kitchen and Leahy is in song.) We have a man and wife who are doing the house chores. This morning we had eggs for breakfast—It is amusing to realize how many times we have gone through this same business of setting up housekeeping, always the problems are basically the same and yet there are constantly new angles and elements.

You have talked about how beautiful it is to think of life together again. I see clearly that in our years together my work has crowded out many other things. Perhaps it is better that this has been true, for our uninterrupted hours together have been so few in comparison to those of others that perhaps the beauty of companionship has been heightened—just as this year of separation has placed great value upon the time of our reunion.

I cannot see myself again being impaled upon a swivel chair's routine, and propose to make every effort to see that those elements of living that are on the fringe of beauty and contemplation shall not be sacrificed—Yes, I shall hope to come with you to Italy and to show you every bit of it and every person. And to England, too. And many other places.

God willing, we shall share the richness of life that He has provided; we shall share it, not by running away from it, but by seeking its every meaning, in the vigor of work, in the quiet of contemplation, in the refreshment of repose. I hope I have not promised you and myself too much, but this is the basis of my present thought and I hope tells you what I had in mind to say tonight.

Tonight I am thinking of Lewis Mountain Road and Charlottesville—I am thinking that in some ways I miss it more than I do our house in Nashville. I think that is all tied up with what I have been writing. It has something to do with purpose in life, but also it is such a rich and beautiful memory of our own intimate living, you and I and the girls.

Devotedly,
Colie

Colie to Ann

Italy
Friday, August 4, 1944

My dearest—

My reading has caught up somewhat of recent date. Read and enjoyed *A Bell for Adano*. It is a great story, though I would not be inclined to put too much emphasis on its accuracy. I would say it was more an impression than a true account, although of course I would not want to speak as an expert on Sicily and Sicilian towns and people. I do feel it is accurate to say that circumstances there and on the mainland are quite dissimilar; the problems there were, in a sense, simpler, perhaps more clearly defined. Here I think there have been conditions that would be expected with a more adult, intelligent, shrewd people.

Yesterday I was frustrated in reading Hugh Walpole's *Katherine Christian*. A beautiful story, in many ways the English *Gone With the Wind*, and it was a tragedy he was not able to finish it. Bought some English copies of Shelley and Keats and find reading them on Italian soil makes a great deal of difference—I've even been so full of energy as to resume a more scholastic approach to the Italian language and have been taking some lessons. To my pleasure I find I know more of the language than I thought.

All my heart,
Colie

On August 4, the British Eighth Army entered Florence. About this time, Colie was in Pietralunga.

Colie to Ann

Monday, August 7, 1944

My dearest—

One experience that now strikes me as amusing, but at the time seemed painful, was in a town where I was living in the city hall, and arranged to have my meals prepared in a family's kitchen. Every meal I ate was with the full attendance of the family who felt it was necessary as a matter of hospitality to attend me, although I find there is nothing more unsettling than eating for an audience. But they were so very nice I couldn't do anything but take it, and I was able to get hot meals by using their stove.

I've naturally been very interested to read of Dewey's nomination and will hope to read about the Democratic convention soon. I can't help but still be a Roosevelt man because I have such complete confidence in his foreign policy. I feel as I always have that it is unfortunate from every angle to have one man in office for such a time, but that we have been tremendously fortunate to have Mr. Roosevelt in these times.

With all my heart,
Colie

Ann to Colie

Nashville
Sunday, August 6, 1944

Darling—

So much is happening in this house now I hardly know which way I am going. Briggs was due to be here another week—but yesterday he had a call telling him to get back as soon as he could get transportation. It was a shock to realize his days were so numbered. This blasted war is just one goodbye after another. In addition to getting Briggs off, I am getting ready to push off with the girls. We leave Tuesday and will be back home on August 22.

Ann

Ann to Colie

Sea Island, Georgia
Thursday, August 10, 1944

Darling—

Here we are finally at Sea Island—we left home Tuesday morning at 10:00—arriving here the next morning early—the girls are being very good—but this twenty-four hour nursing is rather strenuous—

especially when you can't turn them out to graze as one would at home. This hotel is glorious—and should be an ideal spot for the two of us after the war is over. The place is full of army now. It rained most of yesterday but we were finally able to hit the beach later in the afternoon—the girls went wild—dashing into the water and playing in the waves. The sun is out in full glory today—so we spent about two hours at the beach this morning. Now we have finished lunch—and I am trying to get them to take a nap while I get this off to you. The food is excellent—the only trouble being that one is apt to eat too much. The Gardners are good company. We have a charming room overlooking the garden—rather small for two beds and a cot—but we manage—and the children are loving it. I'm afraid I'm missing you too much. Also it was rather bad telling Briggs goodbye—there are times when the essence of war weighs heavily upon me.

Ann

Colie to Ann

Italy
Friday, August 11, 1944

My dearest—

Our drivers have found a piano in the house across the road, one of them plays well and the others sing, and they are putting on a songfest that sounds very gala. This afternoon one of my colleagues, Capt. Riley, and I went for tea with an American woman whose name was Conger and her husband. She has appreciated very much seeing an American again, is consuming copies of *Time* and *Newsweek*, and has asked for copies of the *Tennessean* which I plan to let her have tomorrow.

Our food situation was getting bad, what with the inability of our cook to make sense out of the rations, so I have taken it over. It is surprising what results I am getting. My prime achievement was two meat dishes. We have dehydrated Armour beef that my driver told me was inedible, and bully beef which is the lowest concoction of the war—so, having no other meats, I undertook to guide Alessandro in preparing these. The bully was done in meat patties, seasoned with good strong onions, wrapped in a thin layer of the ever present pasta and fried. Very good! Even my colleagues said so and it is rare indeed to have them approve any tampering with bully. But wait for the big news! The dehydrated beef was used in a shepherd's pie! It was very good. I feel rather proud and even more appreciative of the fact that my colleagues like my experiments, which is no small thing when you consider that they don't take too well with menu-tampering.

My big thought is that you are probably in Sea Island tonight. I hope you have a grand trip and that the girls are thrilled. Best to the Gardners. Kiss the girls.

My heart,
Colie

Robert E. Harwell to Colie

Nashville
Friday, August 11, 1944

Dear Colie—

We have come to the time now when we must make another contract. Sam and I have gone over this thoroughly, and we believe that the contract which we have drawn up, copy of which is enclosed herewith, is in keeping with what Father would have wished. I would be glad to have your opinion of the contract. In the meantime, however, I am going to ask Ann to sign it, for we should not be this far along in the year without one. There might be a great hardship worked on the partnership in case something should happen to any of us.

Devotedly,
Rob

Colie to Ann

Italy
Saturday, August 12, 1944

My dearest—

I am writing in my upstairs room by candlelight. I have a nice table in the corner, a bureau, a good bed covered with netting, a bedside table, three chairs, and a small sofa. My stuff is rather disorderly as I keep much of it on my trunk, but I am quite comfortable. The overall bath situation has been parlous. Now the drivers have rigged up a heating system of woodfire under a big boiler and a canvas placed in a box for a tub, so I anticipate rather thorough cleanliness for a change tomorrow.

My self-burdened job of running the mess continues to be quite amusing. Brown went for the rations today and returned with the most beautiful side of beef you've ever seen. I have long since learned you can't trust an Italian around beef, and Brown knew little of it, so it was up to me to locate the steaks. I'm not sure just what the cut was but we had the thickest, juiciest steak you ever saw, perfectly cooked (on my exact orders) tonight. And French fried potatoes and sliced fresh tomatoes which I was able to buy today. The best meal I can recall in many a day—This seems impossible, but it is also true that I have two bottles of Seagrams VO, so I had a drink of that before dinner, then went to see a movie, *Hit the Ice,* in the little theater used for the troops. An almost civilized Saturday evening.

All my love,
Colie

Ann to Colie

Sea Island, Georgia
Sunday, August 13, 1944

Darling—

It is now Sunday night about 9:30. The girls have just gotten to sleep and I am sitting on the side of my bed writing this because the only available straight chair is being used for the dolls' bed. Yes, we had to bring the dolls and, believe it or not, this morning they went to the beach for an airing.

This place is full of Navy on the weekends—a base near here— saw Guilford Dudley last night.

We are having a wonderful time going in the water. As soon as our breakfast is settled we make a straight line for the beach—staying there until time to come back and dress for lunch—after that we rest

for an hour—I have to lie quietly on my bed to make the girls rest.
Then to the beach again—returning in time to dress for dinner—
have a cocktail in the bar (the girls have ginger ale), then dinner and
bed a little after 9:00. Last night after I had gotten them to sleep I
went down to the patio with the Gardners—where there was
dancing—

Needless to say, I think of you every minute and miss you more
and more. You are always with me.

I love you,
Ann

Colie to Ann

Italy
Tuesday, August 15, 1944

My dearest—

One of our neighbors was in for a session with Capt. Riley and
myself after dinner. He and Riley partook of orange squash and I had
a beaker of water and vino. We talked of cricket and baseball, of the
Yankee Stadium and Wembley, of India and the South, and then, of
all strange things, our guest turned out to be interested in Harry
Emerson Fosdick. Of course I know something of the old
gentleman, but not enough to qualify as an expert. It was an interesting enough bull session to break the monotony of an evening.

Our American friend about whom I wrote you has turned out to
be very pleasant. She and her husband, an old Sicilian gentleman of
charm and culture, are quite hospitable under difficult circumstances. They have open house for tea each afternoon and we drop by
two or three times a week. She dotes on bridge, so always insists on
playing a bit from 6:00 to 7:00. A good break in tempo.

Some friends in a neighboring unit would like to have a buffet-
dance Friday and I have asked my American friend to line up guests.
In my favorite town I helped a unit put one on. They posted attractive and fancy notices, with the aid of my interpreter, and invited all
the signorinas of the town. The next day they realized their mistake
and printed a large supplementary notice stating they had meant no

insult, they were asking all the families as well as the signorinas—So the whole town turned out, more mamas, papas, and babies than signorinas, but it was a nice party—These people are very correct and invitations must be personally and properly extended—Just one of the many things that adds zest to our prosaic life.

Devotedly,
Colie

Ann to Colie

Sea Island, Georgia
Monday, August 21, 1944

My dearest—

We leave here tonight at 9:20—it has been wonderful until the last two days when both girls came down with colds—Carolyn scared me to death last night with a raging temperature—but she woke up this morning with practically none—so I am much relieved. I felt frantic last night in a hotel in a strange town with a strange doctor—who I felt was not particularly competent. The Gardners have been wonderful—but now I am eager to get on the train and get home.

Devotedly,
Ann

CHAPTER TWENTY-TWO

Heartbreaking News

Robert E. Harwell to Colie

Nashville

Monday, August 21, 1944

Dear Colie—

I am writing you today the same letter, one V-mail and one airmail, so that you may get the news as soon as possible.

Last Thursday evening, we had a gathering at Sam's house. Those present were the Howells, the Henry Goodpastures, and myself. Sam ate a hearty dinner, and after I left he began feeling badly. Mort and Sister called Dr. Manier to drop by the house to see him. Dr. Manier thought it best to take him to the hospital where he diagnosed the case as coronary thrombosis. The treatment for that is to be kept very quiet at the hospital for a period of about two weeks and then additional rest at home.

I know how shocked you are going to be when you have this letter, and I am sorry that there is not some way to give you the news so that it will be easier and so that you will not worry anymore than I know you will have to. I will keep you advised daily by airmail.

All of us here send you our love.

Devotedly,
Rob

Telegram from Marie Harwell Howell to Colie

Nashville
Tuesday, August 22, 1944

YOUR BROTHER SAM K. HARWELL JR. DIED TODAY FROM HEART ATTACK. LETTER FOLLOWS.

MARIE HOWELL

Ann to Colie

Nashville
Wednesday, August 23, 1944

My darling—

It breaks my heart to think that so soon again we must send you such heartbreaking news. Somehow it was all right for Grandpa to go—he was old and ready—but not Sam. And the part that concerns me most of all is the realization of what a shock it must be to you. I know how much he has meant to you. The whole thing is past understanding and I suppose we should not even try to understand. I had already left for home when it happened—so I had no knowledge of any of it until I reached the station where Mort met us. We got in last night about 7:15 and as soon as I could get the children settled at home I went to Josephine's and stayed with her until after 11:00.

Sam had meant increasingly more to me since you left—always doing little things for me and making me feel that he was interested in our children and standing behind us in everything. I shall miss him dreadfully. Rob is rather a lonely figure though he is being wonderful about all of it as you know he would. Jane is in Vermont and not getting in until this afternoon. The funeral will be tomorrow.

I wish so that I could be with you to give you what little comfort I could—to at least have you know that your troubles are

Sam Harwell Jr.

my troubles—and that I love you with all my heart.

Devotedly,
Ann

Ann to Colie

Nashville
Thursday, August 24, 1944

Darling—

My thoughts have been with you all day—Everything went off just as Sam would have liked it—The flowers were so beautiful and the church was packed with people—Buck Currie held a beautiful service with Dr. Ragsdale conducting one of the prayers. It was a lovely bright day. Josephine and the children were wonderful. Rob has been superb.

My heart bleeds for you, darling—so far away without the immeasurable comfort of your own family around you. They have all meant so much to me since you have left—trying in a hundred little ways to make me feel less lonely—and I love them as much as if they were my own flesh and blood. Sam's going is dreadful—and I feel more strongly than ever that we must go on trying even harder to make this family group something worthy of the traditions that your father and Sam started—rather than let this terrible tragedy break our spirit—we must pray that because of the tribulation we may gain new strength and a new vision—an added wisdom to see life in its completeness—you yourself have so much to give—understanding, gentleness, a sort of cosmic wisdom, and the glorious gift of laughter. I love you very much, darling—you are as much a part of me as my own heartbeat—your disappointments, your sorrows are mine, too— you are never really alone because I am always with you wherever you go—loving you—dreaming only of that day when the time of separation will be finished.

Devotedly,
Ann

Colie's journal indicates that, from August 24 to 29, he and his driver, Leahy, drove a precipitous route from Citta di Castello through Umbertide to Fabriano, and then on through small towns to Sigillo. On August 29, they arrived in Rome. He did not hear about Sam's death for some time.

Colie to Ann

Italy
Saturday, August 26, 1944

My dearest—

I am sitting on the street in this funny little village and seeing the first signs of life—the street-sweeper making an impressive, dusty tour with his great whisk broom, an old fellow with an amazing pair of pants made up almost entirely of patches, oxen appearing from the stalls where they too are town dwellers, a little girl with a wine bottle, sounds from inside our basement kitchen indicating that tea is brewing. I can hardly realize that September is near, a year away from you already past, another started. This morning my thoughts as always are of you, the girls, and home. With all my heart,

Your devoted,
Colie

Robert E. Harwell to Colie

Nashville
Friday, August 25, 1944

Dear Colie—

Sam is gone and I am now living in a world I never expected to know. A world without Sam. I've thought of losing many of those near and dear to me, but never have I imagined that Sam could go first. All of Sam's life he had planned and worked and arranged for others. As Sally White said, "Sam is the boss." My recollections of Sam at first brought me tremendous grief when I realized what an effort he made for each of us and how important he was to all of us, but those sad recollections I know will bring me great happiness later.

Josephine and the children have been marvelous, Sam's friends have all stood by us, and I know that "all things work together for good for them that love the Lord."

We have all been through a great ordeal, but I think we are beginning to feel equal to the task ahead. I know how deeply this will affect you, Colie, and how terribly grieved you will be, but I don't want you to add concern for any of us to your sorrow. It has been hard, it will be very hard, but we know our tasks as they lie ahead of us and with all of us pulling together, I think we can meet the future. Sam is gone and our world is different, but he had left behind so much, and we are all so anxious to see that the things he strived for shall be carried on in his business, in his church, and in the lives of his children and wife and all his family. I expect Father spent two of the happiest years of his life—these past two years— and Sam was largely responsible for this in his unfailing devotion to him. His daily visits with Sam were the source of much happiness and satisfaction to him. If this had to be, I am thankful that Father could have been spared this sorrow, for he would not have passed another happy moment without Sam.

Colie, we all send you our love and devotion. God bless you.

Rob

Jane McKelvey Harwell to Colie

Enroute to New York
Monday, August 28, 1944

Dearest Colie—

We want you to know—as Rob tried to tell you in his letter—we are going on—and our family spirit is meeting the greatest test it has had to meet yet.

Rob is fine—Colie, I expect this is the worst blow he has ever had, but he is going to be all right. He is meeting everything calmly—and with fortitude.

Sam had fine qualities and lived a rich life. I know how you and Rob feel in losing him. I can only say that through these past days I have never realized so fully how terribly proud I am of your family—my family—and of the ten children who give us all so much to live for.

Devotedly,
Jane

Marie Harwell Howell to Colie

Nashville
Monday, August 28, 1944

Dearest Colie—

I came downstairs ready to write you but the first thing I did was to go to the kitchen to speak to Robert Mackey and we began to talk about Sam and Papa. I said I never dreamed of Sam going—but he said if we read our Bible that we know anyone can go at any moment—I felt almost rebuked—but in a very gentle way—Robert is so sympathetic and understanding and shows it in a multitude of little ways—he had been such a comfort to us all summer—always ready and willing to do anything—he cooked a ham for Briggs' visit—he had been to Beersheba with us three times. Well, what I have to say of him is that he is a Christian gentleman.

I have just talked to Josephine. She is very brave and very sweet and I know all her many capabilities will stand her in good stead as she begins to assume her new responsibilities without Sam—This brings me to Rob and the wonderful way in which he is measuring up to this great change that has come to us all. He has thought of everything—has been so calm and serene—just taking everything as it comes—and being equal to every situation. He is thinking and planning for Josephine and the children in every way that is possible and I hope and pray can continue to do so.

Tuesday afternoon Lucy Ann helped Mort and myself get off some telegrams—she was here when Mort cabled you for me—I do hope the cable reached you before you heard in some other way, but I know there was no way to avert the great shock of this message. Mort wrote the article for the paper (he did for Papa, too). Mortie and Nancy came for the funeral and were such a comfort—did you know they are expecting in February—we are thankful that the family can renew itself. Sammy is still in Macon—flying every day— I could go on and on—but must close. This brings my love and fervent prayer that we may all be reunited before many months.

Your devoted,
Sister

Ann to Colie

Nashville
Tuesday, August 29, 1944

Darling—

It is hard to realize that another fall is almost upon us. I am glad for the Sam Harwells that they will soon have school to keep them occupied. I was over there this afternoon—took Jo a bottle of claret. She told me that she had written you a letter—Marie also has written—I saw the letter last night—and I shall feel much better for you when you have their letters because I know then that you will feel less lonely—we have all thought of you so much—not only the family but many outsiders have called to get your address so they could write you. I have never in my life seen anything like the attention that has been showered on Jo and her family since Sam's passing. The flowers continue to come to the house and the notes and letters pour in by the dozens. It is a wonderful tribute to Sam.

Called Grace Gardner a little while ago to have a chat with her. They were wonderful on the trip and so sweet to the children—Ed is superb with children—he and Carolyn had fun giggling together. Our room was next to theirs and Grace said Ed would listen to Carolyn giggle and say that sounds just like Ann when she was eighteen. I spent quite a lot of my time keeping them dressed up and they did look sweet—Clurie is so lovely and Carolyn so appealing with her auburn curls—

They finally got accustomed to the hotel—which was perfectly charming—and would wander up and down stairs alone. One night after dinner when Carolyn had left the table early I found her sitting up very straight on a chair in the lobby talking very seriously to an elderly gentleman. She also acquired a little fat boy of about twelve who would play with her when we went in swimming. With the children there, I found it easy to make friends and we had many people whom we enjoyed speaking to as we went around. The whole thing reminded me very much of a cruise boat—except for the fact that familiar faces were constantly disappearing and new ones showing up. The place itself is beautiful and the hotel luxurious in a subtle way. They have two beautiful air conditioned bars and an outdoor patio— where there is dancing every night but Sunday. I managed to slip down a few times and enjoy the gaiety—most of the time however I sat in the room until the girls went to sleep then I turned on the lights and read or did the family wash. Clurie said Mummy did lots more washing there than she does at home. I had taken an iron and a little board with me—so I was all ready for the chores.

We went to the beach each morning about 10:30 where we stayed until time to come home and dress for lunch—then we all rested for an hour and I usually fell asleep and had to be awakened by Grace— then we stayed at the beach until time to rush back to the hotel and dress for dinner—After dinner we took a short walk and finally to bed about 9:30. The mosquitoes were so bad after dark we always came in and rushed to the bottle of Campho-Phenique.

Grace and Ed read or went to a movie or went out to the patio—I played bridge two nights with some women from Chicago whose husbands were in the air corps overseas—the two Saturday nights we were there I went to the patio with Ed and Grace—you know how I love to dance so that was fun. We all got marvelous tans—the first time in my life I was ever really proud of my legs—however now we are fading fast. Very easy living—the sun was wonderful and there was always a glorious breeze—after a few days every muscle in my body began to relax. We must go back.

Devotedly,
Ann

Josephine Douglass Harwell to Colie

Nashville
Wednesday, August 30, 1944

Colie my dear—

Writing this letter to you is very hard but everything now is hard, so I am going to try—I can't send you much comfort. I will have to rely on the others to do that for you in the same wonderful way they are trying to get me through every difficult step.

[During Sam's illness] Rob was with me almost all the time, encouraging me, trying to build me up in the wonderful Harwell way that no one else can do. He has meant everything to me—you never know how to appreciate your very nearest until you go through something together and Rob has really gone down with me in this loss. Evalina was and is my other constant support.

The children and I are going to get along—the only thing I have to fall back on is pretty solid and that is the most wonderful family a girl ever married into—you three boys did a good job of marrying three girls who were able to learn to love each other very dearly—even if we had no other assets that is an important one. I'm not overlooking the reason it was possible and that is your feeling for each other. We've all been closer to each other since you went away and it's a feeling that has to grow.

We are going to try to take good care of Rob but we are all leaning heavily on him now and he feels strongly that he must try to take Sam's place in as many ways as possible but as you know Sam's contacts reached on in many directions—a great many that neither Rob or I knew of. He did more concrete good for others than most men are able to accomplish in twice the number of years.

Most affectionately,

Jo

Robert E. Harwell to Colie

Nashville

Thursday, August 31, 1944

Dear Colie—

Sam's will appointed Josephine, you, and me as executors and later trustees. In your absence Josephine and I will act as executors. We will have wonderful assistance with Walton Garrett, John Barksdale, and Hilary Osborn. Sam left a substantial life insurance, and Josephine and the children are well provided for.

A question I am sure that's in your mind is Neely, Harwell & Co., in which you are vitally interested. Our first effort will be to see that Sam's interests are cared for. In a few days, answers to these problems will come, for everything does have a way of working itself out, and I think we will not run into problems that can't be solved.

The people here at the store have been wonderful. We have a fine organization, splendid sources of supply, and many loyal customers. I have made one important move, and have brought Bill Harwell into the house. He has worked throughout the store and has covered a great part of our territory. Bill is smart, and I know he is going to take a keen, personal interest in Neely, Harwell & Co.

The McClure's stores have their financial affairs in first class order. Josephine has already expressed the willingness and desire to learn something about McClure's. She has been with Sam on many buying trips. She has a fine knowledge of what a good store should be as far as the customer is concerned, and I think working with Glenn Garrett and me that she can be of great value to the stores.

Sam had his farms in first class order. Josephine has heard Sam talk about his farms so much that she feels a keen interest in them, and with Sam's farm manager, Sehon McConnell, she can soon determine what she wants to do with these farms in the future.

I have the problem now of being the sole executor of Father's estate, and I will carry on to the best of my ability in bringing this to a close just as Sam and I had planned. As you know, Father's will provided that Sam could buy his home any time within twelve months after Father's death. On Wednesday night before Sam's first attack, Sam and Josephine decided to sell their home and to buy Father's. It is Josephine's desire to carry out Sam's wishes, to take Father's house and dispose of their own. Sister and Mort had not rented their house, so it is available to them whenever they want it.

The greatest problem that I know in your mind is whether you should come home, and if so, should you associate yourself with Neely, Harwell & Co. and McClure's. That will have to be up to you. It is needless for me to say that I do need you, not only to see that your own interest and your own family are cared for, but also to join with me in carrying on for all of the family the business which has been left us by Father and Sam. Father left Sam and me in charge of Neely, Harwell & Co., and it would have been a simple matter for us to have continued to operate with no difficulty whatsoever. Now, Sam's death leaves the burden on me. I do feel equal to the task. However, we both must face the fact that should something happen to me, you could fall into line here but it would be difficult without having had contact with the actual operation of the business. No man could be better qualified to enter a business unrelated to his previous occupation than you are. There are angles which will require study and experience; however, merchandising will get into your bones and you will be surprised how much pleasure you can get from it.

You have been overseas now for more than a year. I have no idea as to whether there is any hope for you to get back, but if you feel that you should come home permanently or for a lengthy furlough, you should not hesitate to make inquiries as to the possibilities.

Jane went back to Vermont to get Jonny and Robin. Josephine, Evalina, Leila, and Buddy are very brave and very wonderful. Tonight Sister and Mort are having all of us for supper, and I look forward to seeing Ann and Clurie and Carolyn.

We will all think of you tonight with much love.

Devotedly,
Rob

CHAPTER TWENTY-THREE

Word Reaches Italy

Colie to Ann

Italy
Tuesday, September 5, 1944

My dearest—

And now a word of an interesting experience we had in one tiny town. It was set off all by itself, so it meant finding our own way there over some unbelievable roads. With the aid of an officer we accidentally met who had been there, we started off right; later civilians set us straight at every crossroads. Finally we came within sight of the town and found the bridge was gone. A civilian guided us through an orchard, over creeks where there was little sign of a road, through ankle deep mud, and finally over a stretch of road that would have been better perhaps if they had never built it.

We made the last climb into the village, found a small group of soldiers in the piazza. A young major gave us a hearty welcome and said I was needed there, and asked us to join their lunch, indicating plates of cheese and tomatoes and bread under the canopy spread against a threatening rain. Just then the rain began. We stood in it and got soaking, eating cheese and tomatoes and drinking tea and

217

talking about our mutual problems. He promised us an interesting night and invited us to share quarters with them in the municipio. I set up my camp bed and Leahy and my *carabinieri* established themselves on the marble floor. My host, the major, was disappointed that the show that night was less exciting than he had promised—mostly silence with the exception of two or three machine gun bursts, but it was ample for me. There being no messing arrangements, I located a house where a family let us cook, so we fared well off bully and the usual viands we carried. In a day or so, I felt the civilian problem had been sorted out and reliable persons put in office (more accurately, I had approved those already put in by the people themselves).

Meantime, however, we thought of the one road out, and the fact that the bridge had gone and the fields through which we had come were now impassable. So I located a man who called himself an engineer. In contrast to some people I have met, he was ready, willing, and eager to remake that bridge. He said it would take several days. I told him I had to leave the next day. He said they would start the next morning at daylight. The next day as I had breakfast on a veranda, I looked down and saw the men at work on the bridge. It was not long after 10:00 when we reached it, but the engineer signalled us across. I looked at the logs they had placed upon earth and rocks—Leahy and I decided to try it. It was one of the best bridges I have ever crossed and the workmen were as pleased as we were when we bumped across.

Devotedly,
Colie

Ann to Colie

Nashville
Thursday, September 7, 1944

Darling—

Each day that passes I keep thinking that we will have word from you that you have heard the news of Sam's passing—and when we don't hear I shudder to think how the news may reach you.

Josephine has decided to sell her house and move into Grandpa's—Sam had wanted to do that all along—she hates to leave her beautiful house but the children seem pleased and it is a good business deal. She is being marvelous—but there are so many things to consider—Marie and Mort will move to their house.

Rob has so much on his mind these days I haven't felt that I should ask him about my financial status—but I feel with Sam gone that I must be extra careful of what I spend.

Clurie is well started in school—today she didn't get home until almost 3:30 and instead of being tired—said she loved it. They go out and play thirty minutes in the morning and thirty minutes in the afternoon—so they get some sunshine. Then she buys lunch there and today she bought the vegetable plate, milk, and ice cream. She's having a wonderful time. Goes out each morning with her satchel to get the school bus.

All my love, darling,
Ann

Colie to Ann

Italy
Friday, September 8, 1944

My dearest—

I had a pleasant stay in Rome—spent a morning at the Vatican including forty-five minutes in the Sistine Chapel, my favorite place of all. There were only Al, Main, and I and two Italians and we had time to go over Michaelangelo's work from all angles, an unexpected treat. Rome is wonderful, scarcely touched by the war.

Have heard that Harry Cain ran for the Senate in Washington—Hear that John Clarke is finance officer in one of the finest areas of Italy and I'm delighted for him—

Always devotedly,
Colie

Colie to Ann

Italy
Saturday, September 9, 1944

My dearest—

Yesterday I received a letter from Rob telling me of Sam's attack. For Sam to be so very sick is almost beyond imagining. I have thought so much of home recently but now I turn my full thoughts to the hope that I may be able to come back before many more months and help share responsibilities there. My prayers and thoughts are constantly with all of you.

With all my love,
Colie

Ann to Colie

Nashville
Sunday, September 10, 1944

Darling—

I know that as a result of Sam's passing you may have some decisions to make and I want you to know that anything you decide will suit me perfectly. You will have to make the final decisions yourself and for that reason I will purposely have little to say unless you ask me—I hate for you to have to make decisions when the news of Sam must be such a shock to you—but perhaps I am making much out of nothing—perhaps when this reaches you, you will already have seen quite clearly what you want to do.

I am beginning to realize more and more how this must shake the very foundation of your thinking—it goes so deep. All your life there have been Grandpa, Sam, and Rob to consult. As well as they were able they made life easy for you—and let you go ahead living your life as it pleased you—and then suddenly in the space of four months there is only Rob—just as suddenly the old easy way is swept aside and certain circumstances must be met and faced.

Almost three weeks now and still no word that you have received any of our messages—it is dreadful to feel that you can't be reached—when things such as this happen I sometimes think I can't go through with this business any longer. No matter how badly I needed you I would not be able to get in touch with you. But enough—I will certainly not be helping you with such as this.

I love you,
Ann

Colie to Robert E. Harwell

Italy
Tuesday, September 12, 1944

Dear Rob—

Naturally my consuming thoughts and prayers are for Sam's recovery. With my thoughts of him there are many for all the family—for Jo and the children, and especially, too, for you. I can only imagine the severe burdens that now rest on you as the result of Father's death, now Sam's sickness, added to what was already such a heavy load. In the past it has not seemed necessary for me to think of coming home in terms of others' welfare—my thoughts in that respect have been almost entirely in terms of my own and my family's happiness. Now I must see this in a new light. I must even consider the possibility that, upon returning, I may be of more value in aiding you than in returning to the paper.

Please be entirely frank as to the value you might place on my being there. It is possible for me to make application for release from active duty in such circumstances. I should consider it my duty from every viewpoint to make such application, but it is also true that I should do so with the clearest of consciences and, at this writing, with the feeling that I had done a reasonable part. This is true especially since mine is frontline work rather than in the possibly more lasting rear. It had already been my thought that I would let the matter of release from service take its own course, for certainly there will remain work to do. But there are many eager and willing to do such work, just as I would be and was under other conditions. Now there is a new light on the subject.

I will be glad also to have you show this letter to Ann. For the moment I would prefer to have you discuss it confidentially—if you should give consideration to such a course on my part I should want to write Mr. Evans promptly, possibly even before a final decision had been made by you. I will await further word from you.

Devotedly,
Colie

Ann to Colie

Nashville
Wednesday, September 13, 1944

Darling—

We are very busy trying to work out the school schedule now that there is homework to do. Clurie doesn't get home until after 3:00— then she must play out awhile, then there is a bath, and two radio programs to be heard—then there is homework—and finally bed. Carolyn doesn't get home until almost 3:00 either—so the house is very quiet and rather strange these days.

Devotedly,
Ann

Colie to Ann

Monday, September 18, 1944

My dearest—

The heart-breaking news of Sam's death reached me yesterday. I can be deeply thankful that the news came in a great flood of letters from Josephine, Rob, Jane, and many wonderful V-mails from you. There was also the cablegram among them. Now I feel desperately lonely, full of tears that were better shed with the others. It is my bereavement that weighs upon me, it reaches out from me and touches many others whom I love, but it is mine.

It has been impossible for me to adjust myself to the realization that Father was dead. I knew that I must wait until I returned home to see it clearly. And in all these thoughts, there was the expectation that Sam's presence and personality would make it possible to adjust myself. Josephine has written me a beautiful letter and has said the thing that would please Sam most—that you girls love one another very deeply and perhaps this is true because of the love we have had for one another as brothers. Sam was the cornerstone, more accurately the tower of that love. It sprang from the love of our parents, it was nourished in our home where nothing was allowed to come before our mutual affection. Friends came by scores, life developed individually for each of us, but that haven of mutual love and strength remained. There was devotion and love, yes, but there was something else—the flaming zeal that protected it. Mother was the center of all our affection, Father the adamant protector. To the world he may just have seemed shrewd and parental—actually he was a fierce combatant. Sam had the spirit of both.

He has been my inspiration in so much of life—not just an inspiration but a constant help, a source of strength. Now I pray that I may be able to make good to him all he has done for me.

I pray that I may be able to help Josephine and his children as he has helped you, that I may be able to join in furnishing some of the motive power for our family unity that he has so long given, that I may be able to achieve some of the things he always inspired me to.

Rob's letter came days ago telling of the first attack. Then yesterday morning there came many letters, from Rob, Josephine, Janie, and from you. It was a great burden of news, but all of you were wonderful in telling me how it happened. The most difficult thing was to bear it in silence. Fortunately it was a busy day in this strange little town, and there were many things I had to do which would please Sam. It was Sunday. The little church on the edge of town had been hit and was filled with rubble. I helped make it possible to clean it up and urged the priest to hold services. At about 6:00, when I thought it would be empty, I went down. Outside I met two elderly sisters from a distant convent who are refugees here. I was able to tell them there would be food the next day. I found the church clean, the altars fresh, candles lit. I was alone for some time. I read the 103rd psalm from my Testament—the psalm Aunt Carrie read to Mother as she was dying: "God will not always chide; neither will he forever keep his anger." I could not help and did not try to keep from crying.

I can think of little else but you and home and all the family. It is my thought to give much time to our affairs when I come back, all of it if it seems advisable. I have written Rob of this. Meantime, I am making inquiry as to the possibility of being released from active duty, a possibility for one over thirty-eight with a need for him at home. I do not mean to rouse your hopes with this, but it is right to tell you.

My deep love to Josephine, Evalina, Leila, and Buddy, to all the family. My heart is forever yours and Clurie's and Carolyn's.

Your devoted,
Colie

Robert E. Harwell to Colie

Nashville
Tuesday, September 19, 1944

Dear Colie—

Colie, I have thought of you more in the past few weeks than I have ever in my life. I hope that you have received the two letters which I wrote immediately after Sam's death, and that they were of some comfort to you. All of us here are anxious to know that you can bear up under this shock, and at the same time carry on the work which I know that you feel you must carry on.

I want you to know how much I appreciate your hope that with an early end to the war, you might be released. I tried to pass on to you my feeling that everything here can run along nicely and that I am quite equal to the task. I can also assure you that things are opening up and beginning to see daylight. Nevertheless, I think that unless you feel that your services are indispensable after the war is over in Europe, that you certainly should explore the possibilities of a release.

This leaves all of us well here.

Devotedly,
Rob

Ann to Colie

Nashville

Wednesday, September 20, 1944

Darling—

All I can think about is our being together again—I want to be so close to you that nothing again will ever seem strange—nothing else in the world will matter as long as I have you—there is so much I want to make of your and my life together—I don't want these separate lives that we are living now—I want it to be one and so rich that it will be not only a constant joy to us but a benediction to anyone who comes within our orbit.

I love you with all my heart.

Devotedly,

Ann

Colie to Robert E. Harwell

Italy

Saturday, September 23, 1944

Dear Rob—

I am deeply grateful for the wonderful letters you have written me about Sam's sickness, then of his going. The letter about Sam's death expressed all your fine sentiments, the deep devotion between you and Sam, and, even with all your own sorrow, you were able to bring comfort to me.

I am pleased that you feel it would be wise for me to join you in the firm. That was my immediate thought and, after your letter today, it is my decision. The makeup of our affairs is such that I cannot reach any other logical conclusion. At our ages, with our families to consider, it would be unfair and unwise to place the burden of it all on you. I do not regard joining the firm as assuming part of a burden—it is a responsibility one approaches as a privilege.

I have written my commanding officer of my decision to ask for inactive status. I have received a very fine note from him today stating he would do all in his power to aid my application, and adding, to my gratification, "It will be a sad day when you leave Eighth Army."

There would be no feeling at any time on my part that I had not contributed a fair share of the job here. I have hit these unbelievable mountain roads of Italy for many months, I have bashed through fields where fifteen hundred weights [Jeeps] were never meant to go and I have learned to sleep with something more disturbing than an elevator outside my door. There have been castles but there also have been many more dingy shacks of stone. In all of it, there has been a feeling that this is worthwhile, and I am glad I have heard many officers who've sweated with other units say so. So I feel it has been a rich and worthy job—and I am grateful that the strength of you and Sam at home have made it possible for me to do these things. I have often realized your part in this for me—I realize it more now than ever when I consider that Sam sacrificed himself to the burden that I and others left there on him.

I am writing Mr. Evans immediately of my decision. It is possible that he will call you when he receives my letter—I hope you will explain to him that it is entirely my decision and I feel sure he will understand and approve it.

My thoughts in these days have often turned to our wonderful home and many cherished memories. I think of you when I realize what loneliness there is in my own heart for Sam. There were seven of us in our family—now there are three. But to these have been added others who share our love as deeply as we do ourselves. I cannot realize that Sam is gone; I am thankful that Josephine and their lovely children are there to share our love for him. Through them he will be with us.

I am glad Josephine has decided to sell their house and take Father's. It seems especially fortunate that Sam had joined in this decision, for otherwise it would have been far more difficult to make.

My great love to each of you, with hopes that not many months shall pass till I'm with you again.

Devotedly,
Colie

Colie to Ann

Italy
Saturday, September 23, 1944

My dearest—

I have written Rob saying I would join him at the store and am hoping to be able to return to inactive status. No early assurance on this, but it is a start in that direction. Also wrote tonight to Mr. Evans. It is the only wise course and I would not want to do otherwise. Hurriedly and with all my heart,

Colie

Anne Williamson McLemore to Colie

Nashville
Sunday, September 24, 1944

My dearest Colie—

You have been in my prayers and thoughts so constantly through the past weeks—how tragic the loss of a loved one is, but how heartbreaking, when one is far away and alone as you are—Sam's going has caused me great sadness—I feel that I have lost one very dear—since you and Briggs have been away, Sam had been very, very thoughtful of me and given me much sweetness. He too was lovely to Ann and the little girls; we all miss him.

I suppose Ann has written you that Briggs left three weeks ago—I really think the second goodbye is more of a breaking up than the first.

Devotedly,
Mother Mac

Ann to Colie

Nashville
Sunday, September 24, 1944

Darling—

We have just come in from a hamburger supper at Edwin Warner Park—the McNeills, Teeny, Edith, Gloria Watson, Becky and her three children, our two girls, and myself. We built a fire—or rather Warren did—and cooked hamburgers and corn. The air was crisp, the fire beautiful, and the children had a grand time.

I was very much interested in reading your letter written to Rob—my heart skipped innumerable beats at the thought that you might ask for a release and come home in the not too distant future. You can well imagine what that would mean to me. Particularly if you are satisfied to do so. He had talked to me about it and I had strongly advised letting you make all your own decisions knowing that in no other way would you be happy—that is my one consideration. Of course you know I have never cared for your beastly hours on the paper—I felt that they not only robbed you but your children as well of much that should be gotten out of life. However, that is neither here nor there—what I want above everything is for you to do the thing that will mean the most to you. I should never be happy unless you were—I think you must consider this thing from all angles—and be sure you have no regrets. Don't jump into it in the tension of the moment. That you should come home if it is at all feasible I think very important—there are many places where you are needed but whether you should give up a career of twenty years is something again and should be considered with the utmost care.

Devotedly,
Ann

Colie to Ann

Italy
Wednesday, September 27, 1944

My dearest—

It has been my good fortune to be very busy. I have covered more places recently than ever, have had many interesting problems—have even been able to "enjoy" the life of a foot soldier on trips into two towns. The exercise was well worth it and it was not nearly as tiring as I might have expected after a life largely sedentary. (My guess is that it actually is less tiring walking than riding over such roads in my fifteen hundred weight). I found one town on a mountain top that was scarcely touched, the air was exhilarating, the water almost bubbled, there were flowers still blooming on the old walls of the

Coleman Harwell (far right) with AMG associates.

narrow little streets. I slept in an old resort hotel—where the Germans had left one bed for me—had a spare but good supper and breakfast (cereal, coffee) in another old hotel. So I feel better physically than ever, and my spirits are much revived by my activities and also by the very close touch I have felt with home.

I feel sure you will have read my letter to Rob. I cannot tell just how great will be my regret on not returning to the paper. That will have to be answered by how well I progress as a merchant. The important thing is that I feel there is no other decision I can make. Strange as it may seem, I feel that my newspaper work comes entirely secondary to it.

I hope Mr. Evans will be persuaded that it is the wise, as well as the only, course for me. I have received a letter from him suggesting that I might ask to be relieved of duty to come home. There was no suggestion that I leave the paper. Before I received his letter I had already written him advising him of my decision. I regret these circumstances for him. I write you now because he may discuss it with you. I want him to understand there is no other decision I could make, that I deeply regret the possibility of adding to his problems, that I will always be grateful to him for our association and hold the *Tennessean* in closest affection.

As to our financial matters, it is obvious that I, with the rest of the family, have looked to "the store" for financial stability at all times. I do not disparage my own earning capacity as an editor. As I had only hinted to you, I had declined opportunities with Scripps-Howard which were excellent and I know I should have soon increased my income from the *Tennessean,* but Neely, Harwell has been a great security as well as source of revenue. It is true that Sam was a brilliant businessman—certainly, I feel, the finest of his age in Nashville—but you may count securely on Rob. He knows the business thoroughly and has great balance. He is just as good a salesman and buyer as he is a financier, and that says a great deal. The financial problems caused by Father's and Sam's deaths are considerable, but they need cause no worry, for each was in the best possible position.

You should not worry about our finances. Continue on your same course of conservatism and you will have no need for concern. As in all other respects, you have been a perfect wife in this. We have always spent less than we might have—therefore, my finances are in good shape.

You have had such heavy burdens—I pray you can find time for rest and some exercise, and can put on a few pounds.

Devotedly,
Colie

Colie to Ann

Italy
Thursday, September 28, 1944

My dearest—

Such luxury I'm living in! There is running water on the first floor of my house, I have a lamp that has been brilliant all evening (though it is waning now) and there is a stove in the kitchen. Maybe the last item sounds unimpressive, but when you've had your meals prepared at a fireplace where *carabinieri*, soldiers, and assorted civilians fight to get at the one small flame, you've no idea how good a real kitchen stove looks. I'm continually amazed by these people with elaborate window fittings that call for an engineering conference equaling a Bailey bridge, amazing bedroom comforts with the ever-present pot—but with no kitchen stove nor any recognizable W. C. The in-between step is the W. C. that is flushed by hand pouring. But why all this? A pleasant young lieutenant stopped in for tea, stayed for dinner prepared by my *carabinieri*, helped enjoy the tray of delicious pastries the townsfolk brought in to me. It was a welcome touch of hospitality—up to my ears in the usual problems and as usual, enjoying it tremendously.

All my love,
Colie

Marie Harwell Howell to Colie

Nashville
Saturday, September 30, 1944

Dearest Colie—

Our lives are moving on in spite of the fact that we all feel our motivating power, that stimulus and zest that came from Sam's dynamic personality, is missing. I was out at your sweet house yesterday afternoon. Hortense was staying with the children for Ann—they played upstairs with Mannie Jackson while Hortense and I visited in the living room—she said, "There is never a day that Dicie and I don't think and talk about the Harwells." She spoke of Sam's generosity and help to her—he once told her to have her pastor come to see him and gave him $10 as a gift from her to the church.

Our tenants moved out of Deerwood yesterday. Josephine has Frances Campbell as agent for her house and she shows it to someone every day or so—just when it will be sold we don't know—it keeps us all feeling that any day now the word to move will come, they here and we to Deerwood. She prefers to show her house furnished, and of course it is far more attractive with its lovely furnishings—her garden is so pretty now, roses, mums in bud, and some of the late summer flowers, the red and blue morning glories stay in bloom almost all day. Ann's flowers are wonderful. She had several vases in the house yesterday.

Mr. James E. Caldwell died Tuesday at age ninety—left eighteen great grandchildren, quite a stake in the future I should say.

We were all at Rolling River Thursday night—Jane had the table on the porch probably for the last time, it is now quite cool and fallish especially in the evening. We loved being together—Rob is very wonderful in answering the new responsibilities that are his now that Sam is gone—He is the greatest possible help and comfort to Josephine in the many questions that arise—She is working very hard at McClure's (the Hillsboro store). She and Jane are going over the stock and getting things better organized—and then I think it helps her to have something of that kind to put her mind on.

This brings my love as always and prayers for a safe and early return to us.

Devotedly,
Sister

CHAPTER TWENTY-FOUR

Life Goes On

Ann to Colie

Nashville
Wednesday, October 4, 1944

Darling—

Dibbie had a cable from Alden yesterday which indicated he would be home soon—she is terribly excited—I told her she and Alden and I would open a bottle of champagne and drink it all between the three of us.

Devotedly,
Ann

Ann to Colie

Nashville
Saturday, October 7, 1944

Darling—

I went over to Josephine's last night and read your beautiful letters and it made my heart ache to think what you have had to go through. I have not yet seen Rob's letter though they are bringing it to me this morning. The thought of having you home is almost too glowing for me to imagine. Yesterday when I was at Thayer I saw at a distance a soldier who reminded me of you and for a moment the whole thing flashed over me—and I felt like running after the man to see if it really could be you.

I love you,
Ann

Colie to Ann

Italy
Sunday, October 8, 1944

My dearest—

I find myself quick to establish my own reminders of civilization wherever I go. This room has suddenly become my haven. There is a table near the window and on it now are a stack of letters from you, my ink bottle, paperclip box, pencils, cigarette tin ash tray, can of beer, ball of twine, and—dominating everything—my favorite pictures of you and Clurie and Carolyn. You are a beautiful and lovable trio. Then there is the white washbasin ringed by my soap box and toilet articles. There are various items of clothing hanging on the door, including my prized dressing gown; there is the modern bookend with my three treasured books (Shakespeare, Maupassant, and poetry collection).

I have had some strenuous, very satisfying experiences of comparatively recent date, particularly foot excursions—they have been choice. One place I climbed to was a lovely town on the crest of a mountain. The people were pleased that I had come and they made me right welcome; cleaned up a neat room with wonderful fresh linen; served me a nice dinner in the dining room of the old inn; talked into the evening about their problems; then a solid breakfast of hard fried eggs and ersatz coffee to set me for the day's walk. Another place I arrived with my kit carried by mules and I was given a royal welcome even in the rain. The parish priest produced an unoccupied house, within two hours had it beautifully furnished, including a cook. The finest item was one of his own beds with a mattress that would make Red Jamison envious and embroidered linen. Strangely, some of the prettiest, most lively, and untouched little cities I've been to have been the most difficult to reach. I have been especially pleased to find the people keen, intelligent, well organized, and strongly anti-Fascist. One old fellow who reminded me of a red-faced Tennessee farmer was reveling in quiet delight in his victory—for twenty-two years he had refused every effort to make him cooperate with the Fascists, now he was the town hero.

Always your devoted,
Colie

Ann to Colie

Nashville
Sunday, October 8, 1944

Darling—

Tonight is one of those times when I know that nothing in life really matters except our being together again—and I shall thank God for the ability to realize just that. The pain of separation is negligible when viewed in the light of what joy there will be when we are once more together. I am humbly grateful for the power to anticipate what that time of reunion will mean.

I am grateful for the power to feel so deeply—I have never been one who wanted life to pass me by too easily—if there must be pain I want to feel it acutely—the more that I may understand happiness when it comes. I hold no brief for self pity—to me it is a thing only to be despised—and in all the months of our separation I have hoped that I have given no one the opportunity to feel sorry for me. I hope that even in my moments of greatest loneliness I have carried myself triumphantly. No one but you will ever really know what a great personal sacrifice your being away has been to me—I seem now to need you more than ever before—perhaps because only now have I developed to the place where I feel that no longer will I need to explain myself to you—I have the feeling that there will never be anything strange between us—and I want you home so desperately.

With all my heart I love you,
Ann

Clurie, Ann, and Carolyn.

Ann to Colie

Nashville
Wednesday, October 11, 1944

Darling—

I had a chat with Mr. Evans in his office yesterday—he called me after he had your letter. Rob had also seen him. He is taking the prospect of your resigning from the paper in a wonderful spirit but he doesn't want you to do it, of course. I was in a position where there was little I could say—and believe it or not, I let him do the talking—neither agreeing or disagreeing with him. However I actually agree with him on many points. The most important being—that I think it very unwise for you to make a decision at the present time that will change the course of your entire professional life. You have had a terrible shock, you have been living under extremely unnatural circumstances for over a year, your perspective is bound to be a bit off balance. To see you give up something that you have worked with for almost twenty years and know so thoroughly for something that is entirely strange should be done only after the most prayerful thought. I think you should have time to see the thing in the cold light of objective thought—which would seem to me to be impossible at this time. I don't mean to suggest in any way what your decision should be—but I do feel that in all fairness to yourself, you should not decide too quickly.

Last night I made Jo come over and have dinner with us. We had waffles, chicken hash, and salad—then I got Con and Dibbie to play bridge with us. I think it was hard for Jo to keep her mind on the game. But she will be better for getting out of the house away from her own problems. Right now she and Marie are both submerged in the problems of moving. We are going to store all the things that are to be divided at Neely, Harwell until you return.

Devotedly,
Ann

Colie to Carolyn

Italy
Friday, October 13, 1944

My dear Carolyn—

I have two nice candles that give a good light, so I will use it to write you. There is seldom any electric light where I go so I have to depend on candles or kerosene lights. Kerosene lights are the kind we used to use when I was a little boy at Ridgetop. That was the only light we had then, twenty-five years ago. They had electric lights in Nashville and in other cities, but in little places like Ridgetop we had only kerosene, or coal oil, lamps. The kerosene is poured into a lamp base which looks like a bottle, and into the top is fixed a base through which a wick runs. There is a glass chimney on top of this. When you use it a whole evening, there is no kerosene left and the glass chimney has become dim with smoke. So the next day you have to clean it. I remember that Hortense used to clean them all every morning. She would line up all the lamps on the rail of the back porch, trim the wicks and put in fresh kerosene and polish the chimneys. She would make them shine brightly. Tell Hortense that when I began to use these lights again over here, I remembered her standing on the back porch cleaning all the lights.

Tonight I had a nice warm bath. It had been a good while since I had a warm all over bath so I enjoyed it a great deal. Over here people do not have many bathtubs. In this house there is not one. But there is a small wooden tub big enough to stand up in. If you sat in it the water would reach up to your knees, but it was not big enough for me to sit in. I had to sit on the edge. With a good deal of splashing I got a very good bath. Then afterwards I had a nice warm supper and then I sat in front of a fire. I was so comfortable that I went to sleep. I think I dreamed about you and Lolly and Mummy. I think about you a great deal and look forward to the time when I can be home with you.

I see many little Italian children. They remind me of you. They play with dolls and play games just like you do. They are very sweet but none of them could take the place of you and Lolly. Sometimes when I talk with them I show them your picture. The last little girl I showed your picture was named Lydia. She said to send you her love.

I love you very much.

Your devoted,
Daddy

Colie to Ann

Italy
Friday, October 13, 1944

My dearest—

Not long ago I had a chance to visit a day or two in a little place where the war had been largely a view from the window and I enjoyed a rest midst the near civilization of a hotel. I must say the rest was welcome for I found myself tired after a period of climbing mountains in company with mules and pushing my truck from impassable roads in company with colonels and oxen. The rest did me worlds of good and I left much refreshed.

Now I hear the sounds of shovels in the street which always has that musical note of getting things done. Chic Sales never took more pride in having a privy built than I have here. The orders I gave were for a hole in the ground with a row of planks about it. When I saw the finished product last night I found a neatly built little job with roof and swinging doors—lacking only an ivy vine and I should not be surprised to find that growing when I inspect tonight.

Always devotedly,
Colie

Robert E. Harwell to Colie

Nashville
Friday, October 13, 1944

Dear Colie—

I visited with Mr. Evans in his office last Friday. I had just received your wonderful letter, and he had just received his.

Nothing could possibly have made me feel happier or more confident in looking forward to the future than to have your message that you had already contacted your commanding officer, and that your desire was to return home as quickly as possible and to join me here at Neely, Harwell & Co.

Josephine sold her house to the Jay Wards for a satisfactory sale. Sister is planning to move back to her house, and Josephine expects to move to Father's in a short time.

I hope that it will be only a short time before you will be back here. I am looking forward to that day as one of the great days of my life.

Devotedly,
Rob

Ann to Colie

Nashville
Saturday, October 14, 1944

Darling—

Winter is finally upon us—after two days of heavy rain the sun is out—for which I am grateful, because this is the day of our one and only football game of the season. The Eagles and Packers are playing this afternoon in a benefit for the Ferrying group and the *Tennessean* is sponsoring it. I am taking Buddy and Clurie with me—so know I shall have a busy afternoon. It should be fun.

Devotedly,
Ann

Ann to Colie

Nashville
Sunday, October 15, 1944

Darling—

Marie and Mort came over last night and had dinner with us. Archie had come to cook for us and it was wonderful to leave a menu and have things the way I like them. We even had coffee in the living room. I tried to talk him into the cooking job but he makes more working four hours a day than I could ever hope to pay him here full time.

I understand Mr. Evans gave one of his famous parties at the club Friday night before the football game. He had chartered the whole place as usual—and I understand had about four hundred people—one person told me he had never seen so many generals.

The girls have just come in—so I shall stop and try to get them organized for the evening. I don't know what I should do without Mother. If she were not here to relieve me, so I can get out occasionally, I should be very frantic indeed.

I love you,
Ann

P.S. Carolyn said this morning at breakfast that when you got home she would certainly have to start getting up early. I asked her why—and she said "so I can watch him take his exercises."

Ann to Colie

Nashville
Wednesday, October 18, 1944

Darling—

I invited Marie and Mort to spend a few nights with us while everything was torn up there. So they came late this afternoon. When I originally issued the invitation Mort said—"I'll bring my own whiskey"—and I suggested that I could furnish the whiskey but I couldn't furnish a cook—so Robert Mackey came with them. I told Mackey it would please you to know he was cooking in your kitchen. It is fun having Robert—and the girls are enjoying the idea of having a sort of houseparty. Carolyn has moved in with me and we have turned her room over to them.

I love you devotedly,
Ann

Colie to Ann

Italy
Friday, October 20, 1944

My dearest—

About the things at Harding Place—there are many things there with deep meaning for me. I am sure that others in the family will feel as I do about many of them. For instance, the two small sofas by the fireplace have always been choice to me and I should choose them as my first selection if the lot fell my way. Then there is the marble top table in the library and the chair opposite, where Mother used to sit. Mother's flat silver always appealed to me and had much meaning; there are several pieces of china I thought were gorgeous, including remaining pieces of the white with a dim gold border. These come first in my memories, but I should not worry too much about them for there are many others dear to me and I have the feeling we can almost surfeit ourselves with things. If it proves burdensome to delay the division, you will have my full support in any selection made.

As to the chances for me to come home, I have only to report that the matter is in the hands of "higher authorities" here. One of my OC's [officer in charge] yesterday paid me a visit and said there was nothing to report except that the high officials concerned were going into it and that my OC was prepared to declare me surplus if need be in order to secure my release. His visit was welcome for, in addition to this show of personal interest, he gave me a few pats for good work—which were surprising even though I was prepared to admit the justification for them. Sometimes when you get out on your own, out of touch with your higher-ups, you have a sense of detachment, and it is pleasant to know you have not been forgotten.

This is a strange thing for me to say for I am one of that group of rather proud, intensely independent civil affairs officers who like to say "tell me where to go and leave me alone—I can take care of myself." If a fellow isn't independent he soon becomes so, or dies of undernourishment.

Another Christmas request, a soccer football. Leahy saw some soldiers with one today and said, "What I'd give for that!" I believe Raymond Johnson at the *Tennessean* will be glad to locate one for you and have it mailed from the office. I'd certainly like to get one, especially since Leahy's Christmas may be thin otherwise.

Your devoted,
Colie

Ann to Colie

Nashville
Sunday, October 22, 1944

Darling—

This is one of those quiet afternoons—almost five o'clock. Marie and Mort have taken our girls with them over to their house, Mother is upstairs writing Briggs—the radio is playing and I almost feel that if I looked carefully I would find you somewhere around the house. Robert cooked us an excellent lunch—Marie and I helped him with the dishes—we chatted awhile and before we realized it the afternoon was over half gone. I found that in asking the Howells over I got their dog Mac too—and the poor thing is so old he can hardly hobble around. Last night when I came in late from dinner he was stretched out on the front stoop after having torn and scattered the mat into a thousand pieces. The mat was of no importance—the funny part was Mort. He said he couldn't understand Mac's doing such a thing. When I left to go to church this morning Mike was just coming in to fill the stoker and when I returned he was still in the kitchen talking to Mackey.

The girls are simply enthralled with the tiny doll dishes you sent—they really are the cutest things I have ever seen and all arrived in perfect condition except for two pieces. I told them they could play with them yesterday and today—then we will put them up. Jo has an extra corner cupboard which she cannot use—a small one with glass doors—so I am going to keep it for her—put it in the corner of the downstairs playroom and fill it with the doll collection.

Carolyn is crazy about Mort and makes over him in a big way—she even goes so far as to insist that he always sit by her. Clurie is just as delighted in her quiet way. She is so interested in all her school activities now—even gets excited over getting books out of the school library.

All my love,
Ann

Colie to Ann

Italy
Monday, October 23, 1944

My dearest—

A man ought to come away from Italy either with a tremendous sense of humour or in a straight jacket. I have just finished a fine meal in the best of circumstances, with sparkling white tablecloth, constant shifting of the dishes, very good food, various maids entering at odd intervals to withdraw one dish and produce another. Present were my host and hostess and myself. The strain is somewhat heavy after a day that was busy, because keeping up with the language itself is no small feat, and trying to carry on an intelligent, small-talk conversation with it, at my stage of conversability, is expecting a good deal. The strain was added to somewhat because it seemed difficult to decide who was the host, I in their house or they in their own, so it seemed to be a question of who would leave the table first. Finally it was resolved when he tried to pour me another glass of wine and I excused myself on the ground of further work to be done, at which point they retired. In their behalf, I must say that when they start retiring, they do it rather quickly.

Devotedly,
Colie

Colie to Ann

Italy
Thursday, October 26, 1944

My dearest—

Yesterday afternoon I dropped into the "dental centre" across the street because I had not seen one since last February. (Strange how we get such prejudices, but I have been warned at home not to use English dentists.) This one was an excellent young captain, with a well rigged office. He went over my "work" thoroughly, came up with comments of praise and called in his technician. Together they spent about five minutes admiring the glitter of my mouth, much as an antique phobe would admire a Duncan Phyfe. He was amazed to hear the work had been done in 1931. In return for his treat he gave me a thorough cleaning and sent me away in fine spirits.

Up the street one of my *carabinieri* met me and said an American major was at the billet waiting for me. It turned out to be Bill Levit, whom I had not seen since old days together in Africa. Bill looks fatter and better than I have ever seen him and is the same easy, pleasant fellow. He knew the legal angles and technicalities about my application for release and also gave me some sound advice on the matter. As the result I have today forwarded my formal application which I think states the case very plainly. I have reason to hope that I may hear from it in a matter of a very few weeks; however this remains to be seen.

With all my heart,
Colie

Robert E. Harwell to Colie

Nashville
Saturday, October 28, 1944

Dear Colie—

I can assure you that everything is going along nicely here, but we are going to need you just as soon as we can possibly have you back. There are many things to be done, and I feel that you should not let anything delay your efforts. Of course, I read the papers and know what a tremendous job the British Eighth Army has on their hands. Nevertheless, there must be many more men in the AMG who are well qualified to carry on the work which you are doing. Father's death and Sam's death coming so closely together leaves such a responsibility on me, and I am making this letter as urgent as I possibly can.

I hope this finds you well and look forward to having some good word from you right away.

Devotedly,
Rob

Ann to Colie

Nashville
Monday, October 30, 1944

Darling—

The children are down at Florence Fletcher's having a get together in honor of Halloween. Carolyn was invited at the last minute and was mighty pleased with herself—we had to rush around and find something for her to wear and finally settled on the Dutch costume Clurie wore in the Mardi Gras several years ago. She looked adorable in it with her auburn hair trailing out the back of the cap. Clurie went in her Indian costume. We had Deborah and Judy for lunch yesterday—then they went to the Belle Meade Club where the children go in costume in honor of Halloween and generally have a big time.

Our house guests—including Robert Mackey—left us this afternoon—we shall be lonely—Last night the place looked like a three ring circus—I had the Arneills, Nielsens, and a couple named Martin here to play poker—Mother came in from her bridge game—Mort came in from running various errands and Marie was wandering in and out. There was a constant shifting of cars—the place looked like Grand Central station. I know you are wondering who the Martins are—she went to Randolph Macon and is a past national president of the Junior League. He is a Colonel in the Army and is at Vultee. She had come down for a couple of weeks to be with him—so I asked them out. We had a pleasant evening—I won 50¢—instead of losing several dollars—so it was a great success as far as I was concerned.

This morning at church both Mort and Rob were installed as deacons—Rob looked very handsome standing there and I kept thinking how it would have pleased both you and Sam. Jo is planning to move tomorrow. The house is not yet finished but enough has been done so that they can get in. The new paint and paper makes the house look wonderful. The front hall is beautiful—it is done in gray with white woodwork. The dining room is going to have a paper on it to blend in with the red rug—the kitchen is the most amazing. They have put new linoleum on the floor and painted the walls white—it's beautiful. Speaking of kitchens—we have certainly eaten well since our company has been around. I turned Mackey loose—and he has really enjoyed himself—it has been nothing for us to have the following for breakfast—orange juice, sausage, eggs, fried tomatoes, corncakes, and coffee. He has not only cooked enormous amounts for us, but he has enjoyed eating himself. I think he has had a marvelous time. When he left I gave him $5—which delighted him.

All my love, darling,
Ann

Colie to Ann

Italy
Monday, October 30, 1944

My dearest—

Spent an hour this afternoon reading the *Tennessean* and felt very much at home. Especially when I read in the personal column about you and the girls coming home from Sea Island. It gets me in a very different mood to read the paper—afterwards this world seems strange. Against a backdrop of thoughts of home, this world becomes properly unreal.

Looking for a candle tonight in my varied luggage, I came across a box of Nabisco wafers and I've consumed almost the entire box. Had dinner with a group of officers tonight and afterwards a pleasant bull session, mainly about odd characters we've known in this business. And we've all known some odd ones—sometimes I think we ourselves are the oddest assortment. Most unreal of all sometimes is the prospect of coming home. I have no idea as to the state of my application. My hope is fervent but I find that I cannot dwell much on the subject—it is too absorbing and I cannot afford to build up to a disappointment. Here's hoping, and loving you every minute.

Devotedly,
Colie

CHAPTER TWENTY-FIVE

Days of Thanksgiving

Ann to Colie

Nashville
Wednesday, November 1, 1944

Darling—

The Sam Harwells moved yesterday and had dinner with us last night. Josephine and Buddy spent the night and Evalina and Leila stayed with friends. Tonight they ate at home—but Jo and Buddy will be here again to spend the night. I can't begin to tell you how happy I am to be able to do something to help them. Principally I think because I know how it would please you to have me do it. The house is still unfinished with more paint to be done and all the paper to go up. But the kitchen is straight under Easter's expert supervision. It really is going to look lovely. Marie and Mort are still camping out after a fashion—but they hope to get their floors done tomorrow and move their furniture out of the garage the next day— so they should be in some sort of shape by the first of next week.

How I wish you were home—not only do I want you for myself so much that my heart aches, but the burden of everyday responsibility gets a bit rough in spots.

Devotedly,
Ann

Raymond Johnson, *Tennessean* Sports Editor, wrote Colie November 3 about the NFL game in Nashville on Dudley Field between the Green Bay Packers and Philadelphia Eagles, saying the *Tennessean* grossed almost $60,000 and "turned over approximately $25,000 to the 20th Ferry Group at Berry Field for its recreation fund." He also mentioned that he was searching for a soccer football at Ann Harwell's request. "I've tried every sporting goods house in Nashville," he reported, "and they are as scarce as gold fillings in a hen's teeth [since] all that the sporting goods manufacturers make now are turned over to the army and navy."

Ann to Colie

Nashville
Friday, November 3, 1944

Darling—

The Willses have taken Clurie to the movie—they called just before dinner and she was terribly excited over the prospect. This afternoon her Brownie Scout group went to the park for a hike, Carolyn went to a birthday party, and Mother to a tea—while I went to Thayer to do my Gray Lady work. This has been a heavy week of Junior League duties—but I hope to have the coming week to myself and get some things done at home for a change. I have books piled a mile high in my room crying to be read—one of them called *Mother Russia*—which I have only barely touched on. I suppose if Briggs has reached his objective, he's very much interested in the Stilwell turn of events—I am extremely curious about the whole situation—and rather uneasy too as to what will really come out of China—of course the Philippine show is superb. I am particularly amazed that we are able to fight on so many fronts at one time. Owsley Manier said to me that the most remarkable thing to him was the fact that we have so many excellent military leaders in this war—when there were so few in World War I.

Devotedly,
Ann

Ann to Colie

Nashville
Monday, November 6, 1944

Darling—

We have suddenly had a change in weather—after having it almost like spring the thermometer dropped last night to below thirty and there was a heavy frost—however the sun is shining and it is glorious. I went to the Thompsons yesterday for a breakfast—Admiral Caperton's daughter had come down to unveil a portrait of her father which was being given to the state—I returned home about 3:00 and wanted to do nothing so much as to drop down and take a nap—but in order to get the girls outdoors one has to get out with them—so we went walking instead. When we were about to enter the park Ed and Grace Gardner showed up—they had already been by here and Mother told them where we were—so we all walked into the park—keeping to the bridle paths and having to get off the path every few minutes to let some riders go by—the children actually got some color in their cheeks for a change.

Then we came on home and at my suggestion Clurie prepared a tea party for the children while I passed a highball for the adults. I wish you could see her at work—she really is very competent—it amazes me how much. She made cocoa, set the table, and passed some cake. If you could have seen her in her little short skirt waiting on them—and she makes good cocoa, too. Then they all dressed up in various odd coats and pretended to give us a show.

Mr. Evans called Saturday to know what I had heard and to ask if you had gotten his letter. I told him you had had no news since you asked for your release and that I was sure you had not received his letter or you would have mentioned it to me.

All my love, darling,
Ann

On November 7, Franklin D. Roosevelt was elected to a fourth term as president, winning with Harry S. Truman as vice-president.

Ann to Colie

Nashville
Wednesday, November 8, 1944

Darling—

Well, the election has come and passed—I know you are pleased—I am not so sure I like it—I think my friend Thomas Jefferson would have objected strenuously to such a long tenure of office. Only time will tell. Marie, Mort, Josephine, Mother, and I had dinner at the Robert Harwells and listened to the returns until after 11:00.

Devotedly,
Ann

Colie to Ann

Italy
Wednesday, November 8, 1944

My dearest—

Thoughts of winter coming on there are difficult to carry in mind, although there are many reminders of it here. I have experienced it all the way from the highways of muddy glue and seemingly ceaseless downpour to the buoyant crisp days of clear skies. I have seen many flowers recently, zinnias, chrysanthemums, and others of the late autumn varieties we know at home. They seem shockingly beautiful against war's black, torn backdrop. It is hard to believe that my second winter away from you has well begun, two summers are now gone. Impatience clashes with resignation, dreams are smeared by reality.

Your devoted,

Colie

Colie to Ann

Italy

Thursday, November 9, 1944

My dearest—

I'm delighted with the news in today's paper that President Roosevelt was reelected. I realize my views are somewhat detached from the U.S. arena but I cannot avoid the conclusion that it is wise for us to have his influence at the helm now and that all other considerations in this generation are secondary to our world relations—for you and me, our children and theirs.

Devotedly,

Colie

Colie Harwell wrote in his journal on November 9: I do not wish to go home with this war still unfinished and with a knowledge that I will find home so much awry, but I can't escape my conclusion that I must go if I can. Ann has borne a disproportionate burden in this. Then there is Rob. I know he is afraid neither of work nor of responsibility, but he is aware that his own death would plunge things into such despair for others.

I find myself prepared to enter the most important town before us in all of Italy, [he wrote of Forli, his next assignment]. I feel it as a great responsibility. Were it not for my thoughts of home, I would approach Forli in the same mood of exhilaration with which I have approached other towns. Now I cannot avoid thinking of the dangers involved, not for me, but for those who count on me. Once under fire, I shall probably think first, as we all do, of myself. But until then, I think of home, of Ann and the children, of Rob and all the others whose welfare is bound so closely together.

Ann to Colie

Nashville
Saturday, November 11, 1944

Darling—

I was delighted to have your V-mail in which you spoke of seeing Bill Levit—mostly because you spoke of your application. It makes me much more optimistic to feel that you have had some expert advice on the subject—makes the whole project seem much more probable. I continue to try not to let it take too much thought on my part—because I simply could not bear the disappointment of expecting it and have the thing drag on interminably. Dibbie was expecting Alden home any minute; every time the phone rang she kept thinking perhaps it was he. Then one day she had three letters from him saying it would be quite some time before he would get home. You can imagine the disappointment. I don't want to let myself in for anything of that sort. So I continue to try to retain my numbness—or complete lack of thought.

Devotedly,
Ann

Ann to Colie

Nashville
Monday, November 13, 1944

Darling—

My greatest pleasure right now is thinking about the dollhouse which I am planning for Clurie's Christmas. They are impossible to buy—so I am going to have one made—then I shall try to fit it out and shall doubtless end up having to make most of the furniture myself. I always wanted one as a child and the best I could do was one made out of an orange crate—so I can hardly wait to work on this one. I have already found a small doll piano with stool—only about two inches long—what I want is little curtains—dressing tables, etc. I haven't made any doll furniture in so long I don't know how it will work out—but I am eager to try. Another problem will be to find dollhouse dolls—we already have the nurse and baby but no mother and father. And I certainly can't make them. I'll let you know how I progress. I've even got Dibbie excited over it—having no girls, she has always wanted to fix a dollhouse—so says she will help me.

I'm going in town tomorrow and shall look again for the dolls—there is so little to buy for children now—everything is paper and a waste of money.

I love you devotedly,
Ann

Colie to Ann

Italy
Thursday, November 16, 1944

My dearest—

This has been my busiest of all times on one of the biggest and most interesting jobs I've ever handled. Days have been filled with all

Colie Harwell (second from left) with Allied associates, including Peter Clarke (third from left).

the multifarious details of the job, night comes on early and thereafter it has been a problem of sessions about our work, housekeeping, etc.

Now I begin to feel somewhat more civilized and settled. Have just finished a long session with my colleagues, Capt. Jesse Mayforth of the Mineola, L.I. [Long Island] police who is my police officer, Capt. Peter Clarke, my assistant, and Gilbert Gall, of the British Red Cross, who is doing a fine job re civilian hospitals and other welfare work. We make a compatible crowd and are enjoying the job immensely—even though we have our periods of chaos such as when I have the newly placed terra cotta stove in my office lit just at nightfall and it smokes us out.

It has been a job from the ground up because I found it necessary to move the whole communal administration as well as our offices into the former Fascist headquarters. But tomorrow I am assured the heater will work—who knows, some day we may have light and water! We have pleasant living quarters in a large apartment with a huge combination dining and living room, well heated and private rooms for each of us. We even talk of the possibility of a warm bath in our very elegant, though waterless, bathroom.

My application has been formally made and I am given reason to hope it may be acted on within a couple of months. It is too big to dwell on, so I'll just leave it at that until further news.

Devotedly,
Colie

Ann to Colie

Nashville
Tuesday, November 21, 1944

Darling—

I told Maggie Sloan this morning when I saw her at a Junior League board meeting that I had been so busy I hadn't been able to write you a letter since Saturday and she said she knew I had been busy—so I hope you will forgive me. I might give you a quickie of what has been going on so you will know what I mean. Sunday I took the girls to Sunday School, came home to tidy up the house, dressed, and went to church. Mother, the girls, and I went down to a place on West End for lunch—got home about 2:30 and worked steadily until time to take a bath and be ready for supper—I had Becky, Bob Looney, Lucy, the Wilsons, Teeny, and Ann Light for a bean supper. Ann L. stayed and helped me with the dishes—when we finished it was 11:00 and we sat down to catch our breath and she stayed until midnight.

Monday morning, after the girls got off to school, I worked on the house—leaving here about 11:00 with Louise Hale to look at a dollhouse for Clurie and other odds and ends—getting home about two minutes before Carolyn's hookup deposited her. I heaved a sigh and thought, finally I can begin to collect myself—when the phone rang and it was Mr. Evans inviting Mother and me to a surprise anniversary party for Mrs. Evans—so I had to scurry around and arrange with Hortense to come out and spend the night—Then I had to get the children's dinner fixed, see that they had their baths, finally get myself bathed and dressed for 7:00 dinner—and home finally after midnight.

Up early this morning in order to run the kindergarten hookup, back home to make beds, dress and get to a board meeting at 10:30—which was also a luncheon. Brought the hookup home. And so it goes.

Consequently I am enjoying the peace and quiet of my own home right now—the Howells and Mother went to the play at the Playhouse but I refused emphatically. I even went so far as to give each of the girls a bath—I scrub them myself once a week just to be sure they are clean and the other times they bathe themselves.

Last night when I had been at the Evanses' about twenty minutes the phone rang and it was for me—when I got there Clurie said, Mummy, Carolyn won't go to bed—so then Carolyn got on the phone and was crying so I couldn't figure out what she wanted. I finally got it that she was mad because she didn't want Hortense to sleep in the room with her. So she ended up sleeping in your bed and leaving Hortense in regal splendor in her room alone. We were discussing it this morning and Hortense repeated her famous phrase about how bad you all were when you were little and what fine men you are now. She keeps me hopeful. I get a tremendous kick out of Hortense—I have to have her out every now and then just to keep up my morale.

Devotedly,
Ann

Ann to Colie

Nashville
Friday, November 24, 1944

Darling—

We had a wonderful Thanksgiving turkey last night at the Howells—Nancy and Mortie are here as is Frances Ewing—she and all the Howell sisters were on hand and we had some very sweet music after dinner with Martha at the piano and Mort playing his violin. They have done a lot toward getting the house in shape. The curtains are up in the living room, the rug down and even pictures on the wall. Mort is terribly excited over being back—and I think Marie is working into it better. She has never said she hated to leave Harding Place but I feel that she did.

I know so well what you mean about impatience giving way to resignation. It must if one is to live and continue with the job. This afternoon I was walking down the hall and a soldier and his wife passed me going down the hall—he was asking her what plans they had made for the evening and they were completely absorbed in their own conversation. My heart skipped a few beats at the anticipation of having you back—at the thought of once again being able to plan things together.

I enjoy my work at Thayer immensely. You have to be on your toes every minute with the GIs. But when they feel you are a right guy, they accept you as naturally as if you were one of them. This afternoon I was talking to a group I have seen week after week and one of them looked at me and said, "I bet you aren't afraid of anything, are you?" Coming that way, I considered it high praise. Some of them have heard me talk about you and they always remember and ask me about you. I like that, too. Some days I go there and feel that I haven't done a particularly good job—others, like today, I come away feeling refreshed no matter how tired my feet and back may feel from walking down endless corridors—It appeals to me because it makes me feel closer to you to know what is going on in the minds and hearts of these soldiers of ours who have given so much and yet ask for so little in return.

All my love, darling,
Ann

Ann to Colie

Nashville
Wednesday, November 29, 1944

Darling—

For some ridiculous reason everyone is doing his or her Christmas shopping early—and although it has not suited me to do mine now I realize that in order to find anything I must go along with the crowds—I still have things to do but the situation is at least in hand—the dollhouse furniture is all bought—which is quite something—because there is practically none to be had—I found the only available supply at Mitchell's.

A funny thing happened today. I called Lip Davis last week to see if they ever made miniature beds for display purposes—he told me a few of the men had made them for their own children but he didn't think he could manage anything of the sort now. Well, he called me the other day and said he would have the bed for me today but I was not to mention it to anyone because obviously everyone in town would be on him to make something for them. So I drove over to the plant this afternoon and there sitting in his office was the cutest doll bed you ever saw but instead of being in miniature it is at least four feet long—made out of real cherry with four little posts—I'm going to give it to Carolyn—and it really is a knockout. Lip was so pleased over doing it—told Mother it had started him off on Christmas. It was a grand thing for him to do and I am very, very grateful. I have already made the sheets for one of the dollhouse beds—I even have everything to the roll of tiny toilet paper, the turkey dinner to go on the table, tiny little goblets, silver service—not real of course—I'm sure Clurie will never get as much fun out of it as I am fixing it up—I even have a miniature Bible.

Tomorrow we are all going over to Josephine's for dinner—the children are excited over the prospect of turkey—and it always tastes so good; I don't wonder they are excited.

We have had quite a few maintenance repairs lately—but I hope they won't mount up too high—money is pouring through my fingers and yet I have nothing to show for it—living costs have unquestionably gone up. We are having trouble with the furnace smoking—it looks as though we may have to have some work done on it. It is smoking in the stoker and fills the house—which is not only unpleasant but will eventually ruin everything in the house.

Then there was a leak somewhere in the outside water pipes—we finally found that—I'm getting to be a pretty darn good mechanic—I can even set the time clock on the furnace and drain the boiler—but baby, it will certainly be a glorious day when you come home and I can turn some of it over to you. The trials of modern life are certainly putting the woman back in the home, but on a little too much of a handyman basis.

I love you with all my heart, darling—I often wonder if you realize how much—

Ann

Colie to Ann

Italy
Wednesday, November 29, 1944

My dearest—

Jesse Mayforth and I are at the end of the dining room table with our two lanterns between us. Jesse is writing and sorting out office "bumph" (paperwork, the term being one the British have long used as it is their word for toilet paper). Gil Gall, our wee Scot friend, and big, rambling Clarke Painter, another American colleague, are settled on the sofa reading. It is a luxurious setting, one we doubly appreciate when friends come in from the chill evening and pull up to the stove.

I have received so many letters from home about the good prospects for the war, when I could find no basis for them—that is, for their bright expectancy—that I feel completely out of touch.

Lest I give the impression that I include your letters with these, I don't—Your thinking I find so very sane—that is, so much like my own, which may not be sane at all. For I know you are thinking as I am that it will not be over until I can sit by the fire with you and wonder if it all really happened. I cannot quite realize all that I have seen and done, nor can I estimate just how close it has come to me. In a sense I find myself in a state, not just of suspense, but of shock. Not from shellfire or bombardment, but from the slow, mounting impressions of a full year in a land of destruction.

When I first was shown this apartment, after a couple of days of fruitless search, I found myself being followed by a whole neighborhood of people through each room. One of them was identified as Rina, the maid of the house, so I took an interest in her. I told her that she was hired—then I said I wanted to find another person to wait on table and help clean up. It was difficult to pin down that extra person. She identified "mia marito," and "mia fratello," and a young woman who was willing but wasn't quite sure she would do. Finally I gave up trying to choose, but said with emphasis that I was hiring only two people and no one else was to come in the house. It was a brave though impossible order.

Of course we needed "Marito" and "Fratello" and they were beavers. When I or anyone else wanted one of a hundred errands run, who should run them but "Marito" and "Fratello," when water was required from the well each morning, who should carry the demijohn on two trips—of course "Marito" and "Fratello." And when our guest list finally soared to twelve extras for lunch, with no notice whatsover, of course the other woman had to be pressed into service. Now when I go into the kitchen I find all four busy at it— the other woman making fried potato patties, Marito washing dishes, Fratello filling the wine bottles, Rina doing everything. But also there is Bambina, a pretty little girl of thirteen who seems very busy, and Bambino, a black-eyed little boy of six who is always receptive to a stick of gum.

I gave up long ago trying to sort them out—the important thing is that we get excellent food, as much service as our tableware can provide, the house gets a full spring cleaning every day, our lamps are always clean and ready, tea is prompt at 7:15 and 4:30, there is always a fire in our one beloved stove, and everybody is very pleased with the general administration. I long since abandoned the idea of learning the names of Marito and Fratello (husband and brother of course) but suppose I will have to ask the name of the other woman, especially as tomorrow is payday. Bambina and Bambino are well off with their titles. As you can see, our entire system revolves around Rina. I thought you'd like a view of this Barnum and Bailey-Waldorf life we lead.

I am almost forgetting the very important date—Dec. 7th. I wish I thought this could reach you in time for it. My heart is yours every moment and I live only for the day when I can tell you I love you.

Devotedly,
Colie

CHAPTER TWENTY-SIX

Homecoming

Colie to Ann

Italy
Friday, December 1, 1944

My dearest—

The pressure of this job has been unremitting. This afternoon was so heavy that when it was over I just sat for a spell—water, electricity, food, and you could never imagine such minute problems as came up. Then a stream of soldiers wanted permits to buy wine for their units. They were certain that I was holding out on them and it was us rather than MPs who had frozen the big supply found nearby. Now a semi-quiet evening by our warm stove is very welcome—No news of my release, so that too keeps bobbing up in my mind—Sorry to see that Harry Cain was defeated for the Senate. Just a line in *Time* magazine.

Devotedly,
Colie

Ann to Colie

Nashville
Friday, December 1, 1944

Darling—

The children are both out of school and the house is beginning to fill up with playmates—Ellen has already arrived and Sandra is expected momentarily—we are going to have a full contingent for lunch. The thermometer is down to 18 [degrees] and the children have wrapped up in their snowsuits and gone out to play. It is a constant puzzle to me why they will not go out on a glorious day and yet insist on it when the weather is anything but propitious.

We had a wonderful dinner at Josephine's last night and even with Mort's strategic carving we managed to assimilate the entire turkey. As a matter of fact there was so much to eat I couldn't finish my dessert. Rob had been out fox hunting—and the subject came up as to whether you would be interested in the sport on your return. I was inclined to think you would—and also wondering if I had already passed that stage in my own development where I would find it possible to learn to jump. I don't cherish the thought of sitting and playing bridge with some of the less hardy ladies while the rest of you enjoy all the fun of the chase.

I just discovered the children down on their stomachs breaking ice off the fish pond—never a dull moment. I go on duty at Thayer at noon and I daresay the hard work there will seem extremely restful in comparison.

I shall be eagerly awaiting the mail—since I have not received a letter from you in a week. I suddenly had a beautiful vision this morning before I got up—a sort of make believe—I thought of course I haven't heard from Colie because he is probably on his way home—But the sunlight of another day soon dispelled all such glories—One simply cannot give in to such glorious fantasies.

Devotedly,
Ann

Ann to Colie

Nashville
Tuesday, December 5, 1944

Darling—

I'm writing this in the midst of hearing a Bob Hope broadcast—so you'll understand if it sounds a bit wacky. I wonder if you get him over there. Or are you always in a state of being without electricity? It must seem strange to live in such elegant buildings as you have at times and yet be without what we Americans consider the necessities of life. Or perhaps you have found that what we consider necessities are not necessarily so.

Carolyn is busy now learning how to write her name and was terribly upset tonight because she was too tired to practice and do it right. She wants to do it well enough to sign her name to a picture she is making for me at kindergarten for my birthday—which is day after tomorrow—said she had to do it so I would know who had drawn the picture. She can write it extremely well. I have some little figures Clurie has drawn which I will send you in my next airmail—she is busy now with all sorts of projects—today she has worked out a Christmas poem—which isn't much—but her enthusiasm is gorgeous (as Mort would say).

Devotedly,
Ann

Colie to Ann

Italy
Thursday, December 7, 1944

My dearest—

I know that each of us has been gasping for breath since I decided to apply for release. I have seen so clearly the picture of home that for a time it overwhelmed me—then I realized I could not continue in that mood, I must plunge myself again into my work and let the dreams of reality wait. Fortunately, this job came along and it has served to keep the waiting from being too intense. Your letters have, above everything, kept me aware of what this has meant to you. I know how much greater has been your burden in every respect, how unfair and unreasonable it is to ask it—but do as you have always done, keep your chin and back straight—wish just enough, but not too much—remember always that I love you with all my heart and miss you every moment, that my one hope and dream is to be with you again.

Colie

Colie to Ann

Italy
Monday, December 11, 1944

My dearest—

It is difficult to realize that this may be my Christmas letter to you. And that we are talking now of plans for our Christmas here in Italy. We hope to find a turkey, we hear there are chestnuts to be had in a nearby town, we received oranges today for the first time in many days, there are reports of a special whiskey ration and (most important) I hope to line up some eggs for that essential early morning nog. We plan to have some friends in for Christmas Eve, some of the city's officials, our very loyal staff, a wonderful little priest who was born in America and who has been our right arm in so many things. We will sing carols, meet old and new friends—and think of home. My dearest, it seems so far, far away from this world, yet is so much in my heart tonight. How I should love to look in on the dollhouse and the Christmas tree, you and Clurie and Carolyn, your mother and all the family. My day will be filled with thoughts of you and them. Smile for me and know that I will be rushing to you as swiftly as ever I can. Bless you all.

Devotedly,
Colie

Headquarters, AMG, Eighth Army, to Coleman A. Harwell

Italy
Monday, December 18, 1944

Capt. C. Harwell, CAO, Forli
Subject: Posting

1. Orders have now been received that you are to return to the United States. Details will be given you by the Adjutant, 2675 regt.

2. Please arrange to hand over immediately and report to Rome as soon as possible.

3. This letter will be your authority to travel.

D.E. AMES
Staff Captain,
for Group Captain,
Officer Commanding,
AMG, Eighth Army.

Robert E. Harwell to Colie

Nashville
Tuesday, December 26, 1944

Dear Colie—

Christmas day was very different this year from any that I have ever known. However, we did have a grand day, thanks to the children. Jane had a happy idea to have Warren and Martine and Sandra out along with Ann, Mrs. McLemore, Clurie, Carolyn, and our family. The six children gave us a lot of pleasure with all their excitement over Christmas. We had a nice Christmas dinner and adjourned late in the afternoon. We missed Josephine, Evalina, Leila, and Sambo, but I think it was very wise that they went to Florida. They not only had a lovely vacation there, but they missed a lot of sorrow, which we all felt so deeply this Christmas with Father and Sam gone.

I suppose that the happiest family of all was Mort and Sister, for they had just seen Sammy graduate from his training and saw him get his wings, and then went on to Montgomery to be with Mortie

Carolyn and Sandra McNeill,
Christmas 1944.

and Nancy. Sammy could go with them fortunately. We haven't heard from them, but we know that they had a lovely day together. Nancy is expecting her baby after the first of February, and everything in that household tended toward making a happy Christmas.

Last night Jane and I came into town. We wanted to go by to see Charlie Martin and then to see Ann, Clurie, and Carolyn before the girls got off to bed. Your girls had a wonderful Christmas. Clurie seemed to be delighted with her dollhouse, which is very attractive and well filled both with furnishings and people. Carolyn was particularly carried away with her lovely bed. It's a beautiful thing, almost large enough for Carolyn—a spool bed, nice mattress, beautiful sheets and pillow cases, and everything just ready for a big doll. I was amused when Carolyn began to get drowsy. She went over and first sat on the side of her bed, then removed her dressing gown, took her doll and dropped it on the floor, and proceeded to climb into her bed herself. Your girls are as sweet as I ever saw in

At right, Sam Howell, 1945, with fellow aviator.

my life, and I am so happy that they seem to be fond of me. Carolyn told me when I asked her if she had heard from her daddy—of course, I knew that they had already received your cable. Carolyn said, "Yes, we had a Christmas telegram from Daddy, and he said he loved us all."

After we left your house we went by Dolly and Hester Warfield's, where we saw Mac and Edith Davis, Matt and Georgia Wigginton, and a few others who dropped in during the course of the evening. We stayed there until nearly 11:00, returning to Rolling River for a good night's sleep.

We missed you very much this year, Colie, but nevertheless, you can rest assured that we are carrying on here as best we know how, and that I am always mindful of your family and your interests.

Devotedly,
Rob

In late December, Colie arrived in Washington where Ann flew to meet him. They returned together to Nashville, where he stayed a week until moving on to temporary assignment at Fort Sam Houston in San Antonio, Texas, awaiting orders to return home permanently. Ann visited him during his stay there.

Colie to Robert E. Harwell

Fort Sam Houston
Thursday, February 1, 1945

Dear Rob—

I had two or three visits with Mr. Evans before I left Nashville. He was very pleasant but we did not again discuss my plans. From my point of view, I do not see the remotest possibility of anything developing to steer me from joining you at the store. The only reason I even make it tentative is that I am not yet released—and in the army you do not count on something until it is in writing.

Devotedly,
Colie

P.S. Be sure of this—my one thought concerns our mutual problems and I intend that nothing, insofar as I control it, will keep me from turning to them as quickly as possible.

After Ann left San Antonio, Colie shared quarters with Nashvillian Walter Sharp.

Colie to Ann

San Antonio
Friday, March 2, 1945

My dearest—

No news yet. Waiting is an even more irksome business without you to share it. However, my morale continues to be pretty good even though I'll stay on the incredulous side until word arrives.

Staying with Walter is very pleasant. Yesterday and today he came in his car which was quite luxurious. Last night Maj. Tripp and I went to the lounge for dinner—an excellent meal of fried chicken. He walked back to the bus stop with me and we had an enjoyable visit. I explained to the bus driver where I wanted to get off. He said he didn't know that street, but would locate it—I saw what he meant later when he got on the wrong route. Someone pointed it out and he said, "Why didn't someone tell me—this is my first trip out." We got back on track and the bus stopped right at Walter's door. I'm sure you've talked to Huldah [Mrs. Walter Sharp]—be sure to tell her how I'm enjoying keeping Walter company.

I'm looking forward to hearing from you today about how things are at home. Give the girls my love. I sure do miss having you with me. It was one of the loveliest stays we've ever had, I think, and I liked everything about it. I'm getting mighty eager to be with you again, and at home!

Devotedly,
Colie

Colie to Ann

San Antonio
Friday, March 2, 1945

My dearest—

Still no news. That is the big item of course and it gets no less important as time goes on. But—*pazienza*—I guess it will arrive in time.

Meantime I'm devoting a good deal of time to sorting out notes and getting a number of things on paper. There are so many details I feel will be interesting in years to come, I want to write them before they are forgotten.

Devotedly,
Colie

Ann to Colie

Nashville
Friday, March 2, 1945

Darling—

Getting ready to go to Thayer—Mike here, working inside—more rain today. Did you hear Roosevelt yesterday? I'm anxious to know what you thought of his delivery. There's an interesting article on Italian war prisoners in the new *Saturday Evening Post*—Marie and Mort came over and spent last evening with us—They enjoyed their trip immensely—said the baby was darling—I miss you constantly—and am looking to nothing except your return—

All my love,
Ann

Colie to Ann

San Antonio
Monday, March 5, 1945

My dearest—

I spent a pleasant evening with Walter and one of his friends, an Army musician, William Strickland, who had some extremely interesting comments to make on the San Antonio orchestra situation. We ate at Caruso's, and had an Italian salad in your honor. Afterward we had a delightful conversation about Nashville personalities.

Much, much love to you and the girls and all the family. I miss you every minute and sure am ready to come home!

Devotedly,
Colie

Robert E. Harwell to Colie

Nashville
Wednesday, March 7, 1945

Dear Colie—

Ann returned safely. I know how much she must have enjoyed her trip from the way she looked. We were all glad to see her.

She gives me renewed hope that you may have some definite word soon. We are all looking forward to the news. Things go along here very much as usual. April, however, is the time when we must make reports on Father's estate, and I was naturally hopeful that you would be back when all those papers had to be turned in.

Jane and the boys join me in very best wishes to you.

Devotedly,
Rob

Telegram from Colie to Ann

San Antonio
Wednesday, March 7, 1945

AM COMING HOME. JUST BEEN ADVISED ORDERS RECEIVED HERE. WILL PROBABLY GO FORT MCPHERSON GEORGIA FRIDAY OR SATURDAY SOON AS INFORMATION MORE COMPLETE WILL PHONE

LOVE
COLIE

A few days later, Colie received an honorable discharge from the United States Army, and returned to Nashville. He resigned as executive editor of the *Tennessean* and entered the mercantile business as a partner in Neely, Harwell & Co.

On May 8, the Allies celebrated V-E Day, the end of the war against Germany. On September 2, Harry S. Truman, who had become president after Franklin Roosevelt's death on April 12, proclaimed V-J Day, victory over Japan.

The war was over.

The Harwell family, circa 1950. Front row, left to right: Jonny Harwell, Coleman Harwell II, Bill Howell, Morton Howell III. Second row: Nancy Howell, Ann Harwell, Anne McLemore, Carolyn Harwell, Marie Howell, Jane Harwell,

Josephine Harwell. Back row: Mortie Howell, Leila Harwell, Rob Harwell Jr., Sam Harwell III, David Andrews, Evalina Andrews, Coleman Harwell, Ann McClure Harwell, Mort Howell, Rob Harwell.

Bibliography

Published

Callender, Harold. "Trained to Govern." *The New York Times Magazine,* 2 May 1943, 10–11.

Doyle, Don H. *Nashville Since the 1920s.* Knoxville: The University of Tennessee Press, 1985.

First Classbook. May to August 1942. Charlottesville, Virginia: The School of Military Government, The University of Virginia, 1942.

Fourth Classbook. May to August 1943. Charlottesville, Virginia: The School of Military Government, The University of Virginia, 1943.

Graham, Eleanor, ed. *Nashville: A Short History and Selected Buildings.* Nashville: Historical Commission of Metropolitan Nashville-Davidson County, Tennessee, 1974.

Hersey, John. *A Bell for Adano.* New York: Alfred A. Knopf, Inc., 1967.

Keegan, John. *The Second World War.* New York: Penguin Books, 1989.

Keegan, John, ed. *The Times Atlas of the Second World War.* New York: Harper & Row, Publishers, 1989.

Leckie, Robert. *Delivered From Evil: The Saga of World War II.* New York: Harper Perennial, 1987.

"Overheard at the Corner." *Alumni News.* Charlottesville: The University of Virginia, May 1942.

Rosenfeld, Louis, M.D. *The Fighting 300th: A History of the Vanderbilt Medical Unit During World War II.* Nashville: Vanderbilt University Medical Center, 1985.

Sherman, Joe. *A Thousand Voices: The Story of Nashville's Union Station.* Nashville, Tennessee: Rutledge Hill Press, 1987.

Stokesbury, James L. *A Short History of World War II.* New York: William Morrow and Company, Inc., 1980.

Sulzberger, C. L. *World War II.* New York: American Heritage, 1989.

Unpublished

Harwell Family letters. May 1943 to March 1945.

Mavis, Stephen F. O. "Reminiscences of Allied Military Government Under Two Flags in Sicily-Italy (1943–1947)" n.d.

Interviews

Harwell, Robert E., Jr.

Howell, Morton B., Jr.

Smith, Alden H.

Wells, Wyatt C., Ph.D.

About the Editor

Ann Harwell Wells, who is known to her family as "Clurie," a daughter of Ann and Coleman Harwell, was born in New York City, and moved to Nashville, Tennessee, at an early age. She earned her bachelor's and master's degrees from Vanderbilt University, and taught three years at the Ensworth School in Nashville. Wells is a writer and editor who also serves as publisher of Backbone Press. She is the author of *Ensworth: The First Twenty-five Years*. She is also a collector and dealer in early Tennessee maps, and has published extensive bibliographies of those maps in the *Tennessee Historical Quarterly*. Her active involvement in the Nashville community has included serving as a member of Leadership Nashville, Regent of the Ladies' Hermitage Association, president of Friends of Vanderbilt's Jean and Alexander Heard Library, and co-chair of the Swan Ball. Wells currently acts as a coordinator of the Reach to Recovery program for the American Cancer Society. She serves on the boards of Ensworth School, Richland Place, and the West End Home, and is president of the Review Club. Ann Wells and her husband, Charles, reside in Nashville, Tennessee, and are the parents of three grown children.